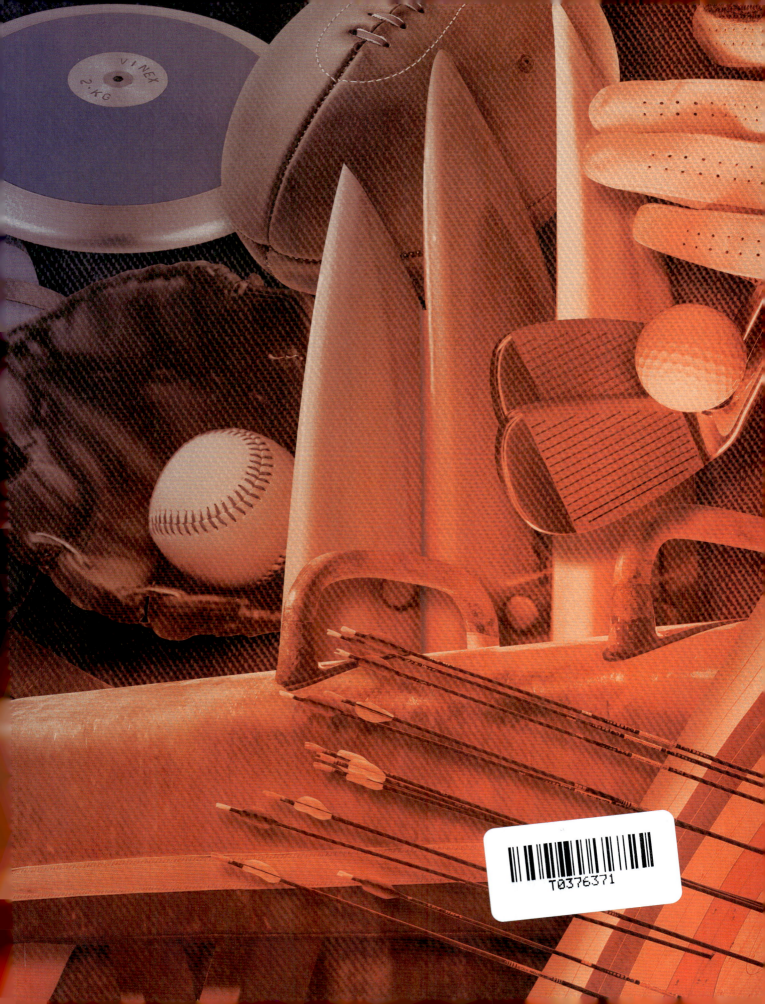

OLYMPIC LEGENDS
USA

WRITTEN BY
KEIR RADNEDGE & AIDAN RADNEDGE

© Danann Media Publishing Limited 2024

First published in the UK by Sona Books, an imprint of Danann Media Publishing Limited 2024

WARNING: For private domestic use only, any unauthorised copying, hiring, lending or public performance of this book is illegal.

CAT NO: SONO590

Photography courtesy of

Getty images:

Pedro Ugarte	Clive Rose	Jamie Squire	Professional Sport
Bryn Lennon	Heinz Kluetmeier	ABC Photo Archives	Adrian Dennis
BlackJack3D	Bob Thomas	Clive Brunskill	Jeff Haynes
The Stanley Weston	Al Bello	Ruediger Fessel	Joe Kennedy
Archive	Agence France Presse	Chris Cole	Gregory Shamus
Focus On Sport	Steve Powell	Martin Rose	Andrew D. Bernstein
Bettmann	Popperfoto	Chris Trotman	Damian Strohmeyer
Lucas Oleniuk	The Asahi Shimbun	Bob Rosato	John Iacono
Tony Duffy	Lynn Johnson	Guang Niu	John W. McDonough
David Madison	Cameron Spencer	Neil Leifer	Icon Sportswire
Saicle	Robert Beck	Simon M Bruty	
Harry How	Doug Pensinger	Hulton Archive	

All other images Alamy, Wiki Commons

Book cover design Darren Grice at Ctrl-d

Layout design Alex Young at Cre81ve

Copy Editor Juliette O'Neill

Proofreader Finn O'Neill

All rights reserved. No part of this title may be reproduced or transmitted in any material form (including photocopying or storing it in any medium by electronic means and whether or not transiently or incidentally to some other use of this publication) without the written permission of the copyright owner, except in accordance with the provisions of the Copyright, Designs and Patents Act 1988. Applications for the copyright owner's written permission should be addressed to the publisher.

Every effort has been made to acknowledge correctly and contact the source and/or copyright holder of each picture and Sona Books apologises for any unintentional errors or omissions, which will be corrected in future editions of the book.

The right of Keir Radnedge to be identified as Author of this Work has been asserted by him in accordance with the Copyright, Designs and Patents Act 1988.

Made in EU.

ISBN: 978-1-915343-51-2

CONTENTS

INTRODUCTION..................9

ARCHERY..................10
Darrell Pace 12

AQUATICS..................14
Matt Biondi 16 • Natalie Coughlin 17 • Duke Kahanamoku 18 • Katie Ledecky 19 • Ryan Lochte 20 • Greg Louganis 21 • Pat McCormick 22 • John Naber 23 • Michael Phelps 24 • Don Schollander 25 • Mark Spitz 26 • Jenny Thompson 26 • Dara Torres 27 • Amy Van Dyken 28 • Johnny Weissmuller 29

BASKETBALL..................30
Carmelo Anthony 32 • Charles Barkley 33 • Larry Bird 34 • Sue Bird 35 • Kobe Bryant 36 • Teresa Edwards 36 • LeBron James 37 • Earvin "Magic" Johnson 39 • Michael Jordan 39 • Lisa Leslie 39

BOXING..................40
Cassius Clay 42 • George Foreman 43 • Joe Frazier 44 • Oscar De La Hoya 45 • Eddie Eagan 46 • "Sugar" Ray Leonard 46 • Floyd Patterson 47

FOOTBALL..................48
Brandi Chastain 50 • Mia Hamm 51 • Kristine Lilly 52 • Megan Rapinoe 52 • Abby Wambach 53

GOLF..................54
Margaret Abbott 56 • Nelly Korda 57 • Charles Sands 58 • Xander Schauffele 59

GYMNASTICS..................60
Simone Biles 62 • Gabby Douglas 63 • George Eyser 64 • Shannon Miller 65 • Carly Patterson 66 • Mary Lou Retton 66 • Kerri Strug 67

RUGBY..................68
Morris Kirksey 70

SHOOTING..................72
Willis A. Lee 74 • Lanny Bassham 75 • Margaret Murdoch 76 • Carl Osburn 76 • Kim Rhode 77

SOFTBALL..................78
Lisa Fernandez 80 • Jennie Finch 81

SURFING..................82
Carissa Moore 84

TENNIS..................86
Andre Agassi 88 • Jennifer Capriati 89 • Serena Williams 90 • Venus Williams 91

TRACK AND FIELD..................92
Evelyn Ashford 94 • Bob Beamon 95 • Joan Benoit 96 • Valerie Brisco-Hooks 97 • Thomas Burke 98 • James Connolly 99 • Ray Ewry 100 • Gail Devers 101 • Allyson Felix 102 • Dick Fosbury 103 • Justin Gatlin 104 • Maurice Greene 105 • Florence Griffith Joyner 106 • Bruce Jenner 106 • Michael Johnson 107 • Jackie Joyner-Kersee 108 • Carl Lewis 108 • Bob Mathias 109 • Bobby Morrow 110 • Edwin Moses 110 • Parry O'Brien 111 • Al Oerter 112 • Jesse Owens 112 • Bob Richards 113 • Ralph Rose 114 • Wilma Rudolph 114 • Mel Sheppard 115 • Tommie Smith 116 • Jim Thorpe 116 • Wyomia Tyus 117 • Mal Whitfield 118 • Lauryn Williams 118 • Babe Didrikson Zaharias 119

VOLLEYBALL..................120
Karch Kiraly 122 • Misty May-Treanor 123 • Kerri Walsh Jennings 124

WRESTLING..................126
Dan Gable 128 • Rulon Gardner 129

OLYMPIC LEGENDS FROM THE REST OF THE WORLD....130
Kenenisa Bekele 132 • Fanny Blankers-Koen 132 • Usain Bolt 133 • Nadia Comăneci 133 • Mo Farah 134 • Birgit Fischer 134 • Aladár Gerevich 135 • Chris Hoy 135 • Sawao Katō 136 • Jason Kenny 136 • Larisa Latynina 137 • Paavo Nurmi 137 • László Papp 138 • Steve Redgrave 138 • David Rudisha 139 • Teófilo Stevenson 139 • Daley Thompson 140 • Laura Trott 140 • Bradley Wiggins 141 • Emil Zátopek 141

INTRODUCTION

The Olympic Games is the world's greatest sporting extravaganza. Every four years some 10,500 athletes match talent and ambition, fuelled by personal and national pride, in two weeks of daily dramas which transfix the planet.

Each Games sees its Olympic Flame sparked into life in ancient Olympia in Greece, home of the original competition in BC776. The original Games attracted widespread popularity across the city states of Greece and lasted until 393 AD when they were discontinued by the Romans. Emperor Theodosius considered the Games a pagan festival.

Nearly 1,400 years later a young Frenchman named Baron Pierre de Coubertin travelled to England and the United States. The popularity of competitive sport in schools, colleges and clubs persuaded him that sporting competition would be beneficial not only for his country and its youth in particular but the world in general.

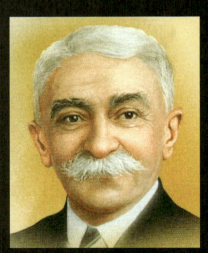

In 1894, still only 31, he summoned a conference at the University of the Sorbonne in Paris which founded the

ABOVE: Pierre de Coubertin

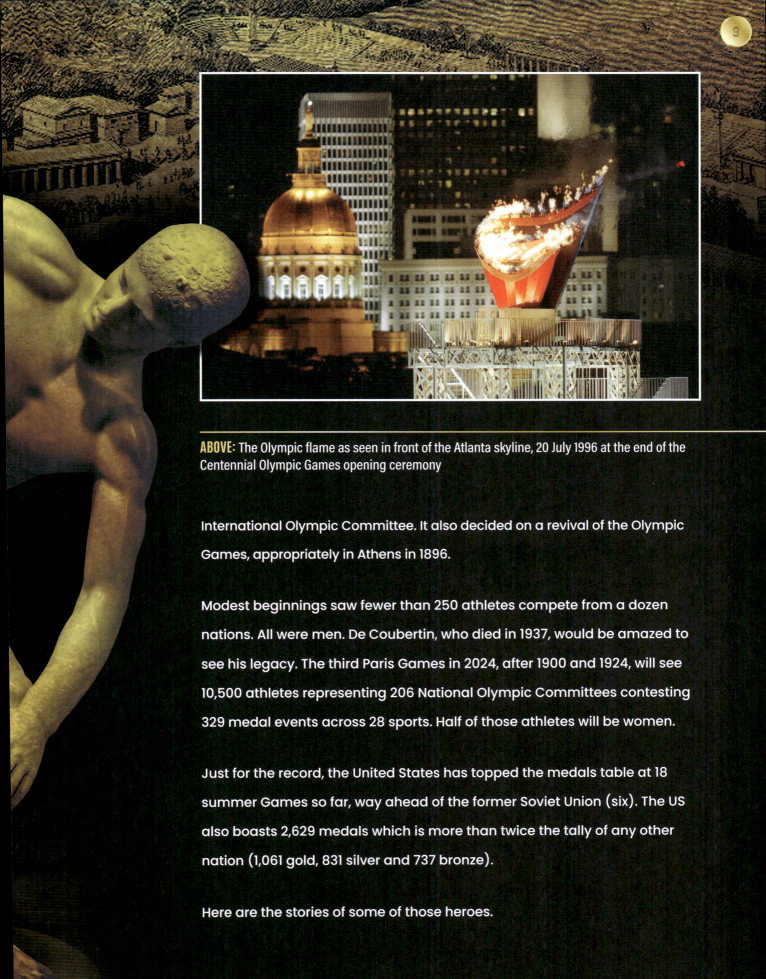

ABOVE: The Olympic flame as seen in front of the Atlanta skyline, 20 July 1996 at the end of the Centennial Olympic Games opening ceremony

International Olympic Committee. It also decided on a revival of the Olympic Games, appropriately in Athens in 1896.

Modest beginnings saw fewer than 250 athletes compete from a dozen nations. All were men. De Coubertin, who died in 1937, would be amazed to see his legacy. The third Paris Games in 2024, after 1900 and 1924, will see 10,500 athletes representing 206 National Olympic Committees contesting 329 medal events across 28 sports. Half of those athletes will be women.

Just for the record, the United States has topped the medals table at 18 summer Games so far, way ahead of the former Soviet Union (six). The US also boasts 2,629 medals which is more than twice the tally of any other nation (1,061 gold, 831 silver and 737 bronze).

Here are the stories of some of those heroes.

ARCHERY

Using a bow to fire arrows has been dated back to the 13th century and Genghis Khan's army, though archery as a sport is thought to have started as an Anglo-French event. It made a debut Olympics appearance at the 1900 Games in Paris but disputes over differing systems of rules meant a 52-year absence between 1920 and 1972. From 1988 onwards there were men's and women's individual and team events, with a mixed team event added at Tokyo 2020.

DARRELL PACE

South Koreans have dominated archery at the Summer Olympics since the country hosted the Games in Seoul in 1988, the year team events were added. But when the World Archery Federation marked its 80th anniversary in 2011, it was an American they chose as "Archer Of The Century". This was Darrell Pace, who took gold in both Montreal in 1976 and Los Angeles four years later. He had been picked for the US team in 1980 but missed out through his country's boycott of the Moscow Games. He went on to add silver in 1988, alongside Jay Barrs and Richard McKinney. The Americans went into the final round, aiming arrows at a board from the furthest distance of 90m, in the lead by two points but were beaten to gold at the last by South Korea's Chun In-soo, Lee Han-sup and Park Sung-soo. Pace and McKinney were long-time rivals – starting with 16-year-old Pace pipping McKinney to a place on the USA's World Archer Championships team by one point during qualifying trials. The USA's first Olympics gold medallist in archery was John Williams in Munich in 1972, setting a record of a total 2,258 points – with Pace falling just 17 points short of matching it at the Games four years later.

RIGHT: Darrell Pace won individual gold medals at the 1976 and 1984 Olympic Games

BORN: October 23, 1956, in Cincinatti, Ohio

EVENT: Archery

GOLD (2): Individual (Montreal 1976), Individual (Los Angeles 1984)

SILVER (1): Team (Seoul 1988)

TOTAL MEDALS: 🥇🥇🥈

ABOVE: Poster for the 1980 Moscow Games - The US team boycott meant Pace didn't get to defend his 1976 individual gold

AQUATICS

Diving, swimming, synchronised swimming and water polo make up the Olympics' aquatics programme. Swimming featured at the first modern Games in Athens in 1896, with four men-only freestyle race events. Since 1924 the official Olympic length of a pool became 50m – as it remains today. Only track and field has more medal events than swimming, with 37 at Tokyo 2020 and again at the 2024 Games in Paris. Water polo for men began in 1900, and for women 100 years later, while women-only synchronised swimming was introduced in 1984. Diving was added for men in 1904 and for women eight years later.

MATT BIONDI

OLYMPIC LEGENDS USA

Californian freestyle and butterfly swimming sensation Matt Biondi was just 20 when he became the first swimmer to win seven medals at the World Aquatics Championships, in Madrid in 1986 – including three golds. That came a year after he was part of the US men's 4 x 100m freestyle relay team taking gold at the Summer Olympics in Los Angeles. Biondi went into the Games in Seoul in 1988 hoping to match Mark Spitz's then-record of seven Olympics golds in one summer from 1972 in Munich. Biondi set off to an underwhelming start, by his standards anyway. He began with bronze in the 200m freestyle then silver in the 100m butterfly, losing his lead in the second race in the final moments as Suriname's Anthony Nesty overtook and won by an inch. But Biondi then won gold in all his five remaining races – breaking four world records as he did so. He retired from competitive swimming but returned to take part in the Olympics in Barcelona in 1992, where he was a member of the triumphant men's 4 x 100 freestyle relay and 4 x 100 medley relay teams, while adding silver in the 50m freestyle – leaving him with 11 Olympic medals overall, eight of them gold. Two-metre-tall Biondi went on to work as a swimming coach and maths teacher.

ABOVE: Poster from the 1984 Los Angeles Olympic Games

BELOW: Matt Biondi reacts to winning the Men's 50 meter freestyle swimming event of the 1988 Olympic Games on September 24, 1988 at the Jamsil Indoor swimming pool in Seoul, South Korea. Biondi set a new world record in the race

BORN: October 8, 1965, in Moraga, California

EVENTS: Swimming - butterfly, freestyle, medley

GOLD (8): 4 x 100m freestyle (Los Angeles 1984), 50m freestyle, 100m freestyle, 4 x 100m freestyle, 4 x 200m freestyle, 4 x 100m medley (Seoul 1988), 4 x 100m freestyle, 4 x 100m medley (Barcelona 1992)

SILVER (2): 100m butterfly (Seoul 1988), 50m freestyle (Barcelona 1992)

BRONZE (1): 200m freestyle (Seoul 1988)

TOTAL MEDALS:

NATALIE COUGHLIN

Natalie Coughlin became the first woman to ever win back-to-back 100m backstroke Olympic golds when she successfully defended her title in Beijing in 2008, after her first in Athens four years earlier. The then-25-year-old was one of the global stars of the Beijing Games, as the first American woman to win as many as six medals at one Olympics – adding two silvers and three bronzes, before another bronze as part of the 4 x 100m freestyle relay team at London 2012. Coughlin finished her career with three Olympic golds in total, having also been part of the USA's winning 4 x 200m freestyle relay team in Athens. Coughlin was presented with her history-making backstroke gold in Beijing while her lip was still bleeding as she stood on the podium – she had bitten it during the race which she led from the start, to distract from pain she was feeling in her legs. Coughlin was renowned for her powerful kick in the pool. She missed out on a place in the USA team going to Sydney for the 2000 Olympics after breaking her left shoulder labrum during a butterfly set – and refused to watch the Games on TV. She responded by opting against surgery and knuckling down to whole workouts doing nothing but kicking. Since her Beijing triumphs she has also taken part in TV cooking shows and America's *Dancing With The Stars* series.

BORN: August 23, 1982, in Vallejo, California

EVENTS: Swimming – backstroke, butterfly, freestyle, medley

GOLD (3): 100m backstroke, 4 x 200m freestyle (Athens 2004), 100m backstroke (Beijing 2008)

SILVER (4): 4 x 100m freestyle, 4 x 100m medley (Athens 2004), 4 x 100m freestyle, 4 x 100m medley (Beijing 2008)

BRONZE (5): 100m freestyle (Athens 2004), 100m freestyle, 200m medley, 4 x 200m freestyle (Beijing 2008), 4 x 100m freestyle (London 2012)

DUKE KAHANAMOKU

Hawaii's Duke Kahanamoku has gone down as both a swimming and surfing legend. He was born and brought up in Hawaii, where he would surf off the coast of Waikiki as a teenager with a 5m-long, 52kg board he built from the wood of a koa tree. His powerful swimming also made waves and he won the first of his three Olympic golds in the 100m freestyle at Stockholm in 1912 – though not without a scare first. He and fellow US team members Kenneth Huszagh and Perry McGillivray failed to make it to the semi-finals but were given another chance to make the final in an extra heat, but told they would have to beat the 1:06.2 time of Billy Longworth, who finished third in the initial race. Kahanamoku not only did so but also matched Kurt Bretting's world record of 1:02.4, before comfortably winning the final in 1:03.4. He won again eight years later in Antwerp, this time setting a record of 1:01.4 – but finished second to future Tarzan star Johnny Weissmuller in Paris four years later, with Duke's brother Samuel Kahanamoku winning bronze. Duke's surfing exhibitions both in the USA and Australia after retirement are said to have helped popularise it as a sport and an activity. He also used his board to help save eight passengers when a boat capsized off the beach at Corona del Mar in California in June 1925, although 17 people died.

ABOVE: A poster by artist Olle Hjortzberg for the 1912 Summer Olympics held in Stockholm

BELOW: Duke Paoa Kahanamoku with his surfboard, c. 1910-1915

BORN: August 24, 1890, in Honolulu, Hawaii

DIED: January 22, 1968, aged 77, in Honolulu, Hawaii

EVENT: Swimming – freestyle

GOLD (3): 100m freestyle (Stockholm 1912), 100m freestyle, 4 x 200m freestyle relay (Antwerp 1920)

SILVER (2): 4 x 200m freestyle relay (Stockholm 1912), 100m freestyle (Paris 1924)

TOTAL MEDALS: 🥇🥇🥇🥈🥈

AQUATICS

KATIE LEDECKY

No woman has won more Olympic swimming golds than ever-consistent Katie Ledecky's seven – not to mention her three silvers, as well as 21 World Aquatics Championships golds and five silvers. She made her Summer Games breakthrough with 800m freestyle gold at London 2012, finishing the final in a time of 8:14.63 – more than four seconds clear of closest challenger Mireia Belmonte García from Spain. Great Britain's defending champion Rebecca Adlington came third. Only Adlington's winning time of 8:14.10 in Beijing four years earlier was faster than Ledecky's London triumph. Ledecky would set two records of her own in Rio in 2016, winning 400m freestyle gold in 3:56.46 and in the 800m freestyle at 8:04.79 – she also added golds in the 200m freestyle and 4 x 200m freestyle relay. She lost an individual Olympics final for the first time at the delayed 2020 Games in Tokyo in 2021, finishing second behind Australia's Ariarne Titmus in the 400m freestyle. However, Ledecky bounced back to win a pair of golds at longer distances – the 800m freestyle and 1500m freestyle, making her the most successful US female competitor for the second consecutive Games. Despite her immense success, she insists she "never really aims for medal-count records" – and was often seen keenly checking on her US colleagues as soon as she herself had finished first.

BORN: March 17, 1997, in Washington, D.C.

EVENT: Swimming - freestyle

GOLD (7): 800m freestyle (London 2012), 200m freestyle, 400m freestyle, 800m freestyle, 4 x 200m freestyle relay (Rio 2016), 800m freestyle, 1500m freestyle (Tokyo 2020)

SILVER (3): 4 x 100m freestyle relay (Rio 2016), 400m freestyle, 4 x 200m freestyle relay (Tokyo 2020)

TOTAL MEDALS: 🥇🥇🥇🥇🥇🥇🥇🥈🥈🥈

RYAN LOCHTE

BELOW: Gold Medallist Ryan poses on the podium during the medal ceremony for the Men's 4 x 200m Freestyle Relay final on Day 4 of the London 2012 Olympic Games

Ryan Lochte's swimming coach father Steven has said it took a while for his son to take the sport seriously as a boy – telling an interviewer in 2007: "Most of the time he was doing something wrong, pulling on somebody's leg, blowing bubbles underwater, hiding at the other end of the pool." Steven would send Ryan to the showers when he felt he was "messing around" too much, adding: "He spent more time in the showers than he did in the pool." Yet Lochte vowed to change his attitude after losing at the Junior Olympic Games as a 14-year-old and has since gone on to become one of the USA's most successful Olympic swimmers of all time, with golds at four separate Games – though not without controversy along the way. He has six Olympic golds, two for individual events and four in relay teams alongside his friend and rival Michael Phelps, and is renowned for his underwater kicking and fierce pace across short distances. But Lochte's part in the USA's 4 x 200m freestyle triumph in Rio in 2016 was then overshadowed by what became dubbed "Lochtegate". He and team-mates Gunnar Bentz, Jack Conger and Jimmy Feigen claimed to have been robbed at gunpoint during a night out in Rio, only for police to later accuse them instead of damaging a petrol station while drunk. Lochte apologised for having "over-exaggerated that story" and was banned by USA swimming for ten months.

BORN: August 3, 1984, in Rochester, New York

EVENTS: Swimming - backstroke, freestyle, medley

GOLD (6): 4 x 200m freestyle (Athens 2004), 200m backstroke, 4x200m freestyle (Beijing 2008), 400m medley, 4 x 200m freestyle (London 2012), 4 x 200m freestyle (Rio 2016)

SILVER (3): 200m medley (Athens 2004), 200m medley, 4 x 100m freestyle (London 2012)

BRONZE (3): 200m medley, 400m medley (Beijing 2008), 200m backstroke (London 2012)

TOTAL MEDALS:

GREG LOUGANIS

Greg Louganis made Olympic history in a way traumatic as well as triumphant at Seoul in 1988. The 38-year-old won both men's diving golds, in the 10m platform and 3m springboard, just as he had four years earlier in Los Angeles – the first male diver to sweep the board at successive Games and only the second diver, after US compatriot Pat McCormick won the equivalent women's events in Helsinki in 1952 and Melbourne in 1956. Louganis, put up for adoption by his 15-year-old parents as a baby, struggled growing up – he was bullied at school for his dyslexia and love of gymnastics and turned to drugs and alcohol. But he was encouraged by his adoptive parents to pursue diving and was coached by Dr Sammy Lee, winner of diving golds for Great Britain in 1948 and 1952. Louganis claimed 10m platform silver at Montreal in 1976, aged 16, before missing the Moscow Games four years later due to the US boycott. His elegant dives scored more than 700 points in both his 1984 victories. But his ninth dive in a Seoul preliminary round saw him bang his head on the board performing a reverse two-and-a-half somersault in the pike position. After receiving temporary sutures he managed another reverse somersault little more than half an hour later before being taken to hospital for stitches. Louganis returned the following day to complete the heat with the same dive before later securing both golds. Louganis revealed in 1995 he was diagnosed with HIV six months before the Games and was terrified blood in the pool could put others at risk, but doctors insisted there was no danger as the water would dilute it sufficiently.

ABOVE: Montreal 1976 Olympic Games poster design

BORN: January 29, 1960, in San Diego, California

EVENT: Men's diving – platform, springboard

GOLD (4): 10m platform, 3m springboard (Los Angeles 1984), 10m platform, 3m springboard (Seoul 1988)

SILVER (1): 10m platform (Montreal 1976)

TOTAL MEDALS: 🥇🥇🥇🥇🥈

PAT McCORMICK

Before Greg Louganis, fellow American Pat McCormick was the only person to win both diving golds available at each of two consecutive Olympics. Yet the event was said to have such a low profile back in 1952 that when she returned triumphant from Finland's Helsinki with her pair of medals, neighbours asked whether she had been away on holiday. France's Mady Moreau, who took silver in the springboard final, was the first non-American medallist in the event which was being held for the seventh time. McCormick retained both her 10m platform and 3m springboard titles four years later in Melbourne, despite giving birth to son Tim just months before the Games. She had kept up her training while pregnant, including half-mile daily swims until only two days before giving birth. In 1965 she was one of the first people inducted into the new International Swimming Hall of Fame, which has a museum based in Fort Lauderdale, Florida. McCormick later served on the organising committee for the 1984 Summer Olympics in Los Angeles. The mother-of-two – daughter Kelly was born in 1960 – died in March 2023 aged 92.

TOP RIGHT: 1952 Helsinki Olympic Games official poster

RIGHT: Pat McCormick holds the James E. Sullivan Award, presented by the Amateur Athletic Union in 1957

BORN: May 12, 1930, in Seal Beach, California

DIED: March 7, 2023, aged 92, in Orange County, California

EVENT: Diving – platform, springboard

GOLD (4): 10m platform, 3m springboard (Helsinki 1952), 10m platform, 3m springboard (Melbourne 1956)

TOTAL MEDALS: 🥇🥇🥇🥇

JOHN NABER

BORN: January 20, 1956, in Evanston, Illinois

EVENTS: Swimming – backstroke, freestyle

GOLD (4): 100m backstroke, 200m backstroke, 4 x 200m freestyle, 4 x 100m medley (Montreal 1976)

SILVER (1): 200m freestyle (Montreal 1976)

TOTAL MEDALS: 🥇🥇🥇🥇🥈

Four years after Mark Spitz's record-breaking feats in the pool in Munich, the US again dominated the swimming events in Montreal in 1976 – with John Naber among the most spectacular performers. He broke the world record in each of the four finals he won, two individually and twice as part of a relay team. His 100m backstroke semi-final set a record of 56.19 which he then topped the following day with 55.49 in the final to clinch his first Olympic gold – fulfilling an ambition he apparently revealed to his parents as a nine-year-old boy visiting Olympia in Greece, which was home of the ancient original Games in 776 BC. Naber followed this up by winning the 200m backstroke in 1:59.19, the first time it had ever been completed in under two minutes. The US set records in both the semi-finals and finals of both the 4 x 200m freestyle and 4 x 100m medley events, though did some squad rotation each time. In the 4 x 200m freestyle Doug Northway, Tim Shaw, Mike Bruner and Bruce Furniss swam 7:30.55 to qualify before Naber and Jim Montgomery came in for Northway and Shaw and helped win in 7:23.22 – while in the 4 x 100m medley there were two entirely different teams. Peter Rocca, Chris Woo, Joe Bottom and Jack Babashoff achieved 3:47.28 in the semi-final, then Naber, John Hencken, Matthew Vogel and James Montgomery bettered it with 3:42.22.

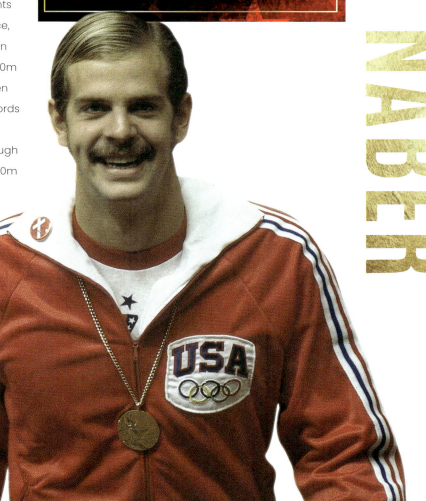

MICHAEL PHELPS

Swimming phenomenon Michael Phelps stands alone as the most-decorated Olympian of modern times. In Beijing in 2008 he became the first athlete to win eight gold medals at a single Summer Olympics, going one better than fellow US swimmer Mark Spitz's seven in Munich in 1972. Seven of the eight set records and Phelps suggested he was the ultimate "morning person" by winning them all before Beijing lunchtime. Yet this was no breakthrough surprise – and nor was it enough for Phelps, who kept on winning and now owns an all-time Olympic record of 28 medals, including 23 golds (also more than anyone else). Four years before Beijing he won eight medals, six of them gold, at Athens 2004. He only missed the chance to equal Spitz's gold record back then when giving up his place in the 4 x 100m medley relay team to Ian Crocker – Phelps had beaten him by just 0.04 seconds in the 100m butterfly. Phelps – blessed with 1.93m in height, 2.01m in arm span and size 14 feet – began swimming as a seven-year-old and was soon setting national age group records. He followed Beijing with four golds and two silvers at London 2012 then another five golds and a silver in Rio four years later, where he was also chosen as his country's flag-bearer for the Opening Ceremony athletes' parade. Phelps – who began his Olympic career as a 15-year-old at Athens in 2000, the youngest member of the US swimming team for 68 years – has made a point of regularly freshening up which events to target and train for between Games. He did announce his retirement after London 2012 but announced a return in April 2014. His aims included reclaiming the 4 x 100m freestyle title the US won in Beijing before finishing second in London – which of course Phelps, by now 31, helped them achieve in Rio, in an Olympic record time of 3:27.95.

BORN: June 30, 1985, in Baltimore, Maryland

EVENTS: Swimming – backstroke, butterfly, freestyle, medley

GOLD (23): 100m butterfly, 200m butterfly, 200m medley, 400m medley, 4 x 200m freestyle, 4 x 100m medley (Athens 2004), 200m freestyle, 100m butterfly, 200m butterfly, 200m medley, 400m medley, 4 x 100m freestyle, 4 x 200m freestyle, 4 x 100m medley (Beijing 2008), 100m butterfly, 200m medley, 4 x 200m freestyle, 4 x 100m medley (London 2012), 200m butterfly, 200m medley, 4 x 100m freestyle, 4 x 200m freestyle, 4 x 100m medley

SILVER (3): 200m butterfly, 4 x 100m freestyle (London 2012), 100m butterfly (Rio 2016)

BRONZE (2): 200m freestyle, 4 x 100m freestyle (Athens 2004)

TOTAL MEDALS:

DON SCHOLLANDER

Eighteen-year-old Don Schollander won four gold medals at the 1964 Olympics in Tokyo, the first American to claim that many at a single Games since track and field athlete Jesse Owens in Berlin in 1936. Schollander's first was in the 100m freestyle, when he overtook Britain's Bob McGregor with five metres to go and finished with a new Olympic record of 53.4. He followed this with another win in the 400m freestyle then more golds in the 4 x 100m freestyle – setting a record of 3:32.2 alongside Stephen Clark, Michael Austin and Gary Ilman – and the 4 x 200m freestyle, swimming the final leg after Clark, Roy Saari and Ilman to achieve another world record of 7:52.1. But he missed out on the chance of a fifth gold, with Clark favoured instead for the USA's 4 x 100m medley victory. Schollander considered the 200m freestyle his strongest event but this was not added to the Olympics roster until Mexico City, where he felt his powers had waned after illness and had to settle for silver behind Australia's Michael Wenden. Both struggled with the altitude and Schollander needed oxygen. He announced his retirement after the race, saying: "I'm finished with water – in fact I may not take a bath or shower for another two years." He did leave Mexico City with another gold, however – in the 4 x 200m, again swimming fourth, this time after John Nelson, Stephen Rerych and Mark Spitz.

ABOVE: Official 1964 Tokyo Olympic Games poster artwork

BELOW: Don Schollander being interviewed by journalists during the Tokyo Olympics, October 1964

BORN: April 30, 1946, in Charlotte, North Carolina

EVENT: Swimming – freestyle

GOLD (5): 100m freestyle, 400m freestyle, 4 x 100m freestyle, 4 x 200m freestyle (Tokyo 1964), 4 x 200m freestyle (Mexico City 1968)

SILVER (1): 200m freestyle (Mexico City 1968)

TOTAL MEDALS: 🥇🥇🥇🥇🥇🥈

MARK SPITZ

BORN: February 10, 1950, in Modesto, California

EVENTS: Swimming – butterfly, freestyle, medley

GOLD (9): 4 x 100m freestyle, 4 x 200m freestyle (Mexico City 1968), 100m butterfly, 100m freestyle, 200m butterfly, 200m freestyle, 4 x 100m freestyle, 4 x 100m medley, 4 x 200m freestyle (Munich 1972)

SILVER (1): 100m butterfly (Mexico City 1968)

BRONZE (1): 100m freestyle (Mexico City 1968)

TOTAL MEDALS:

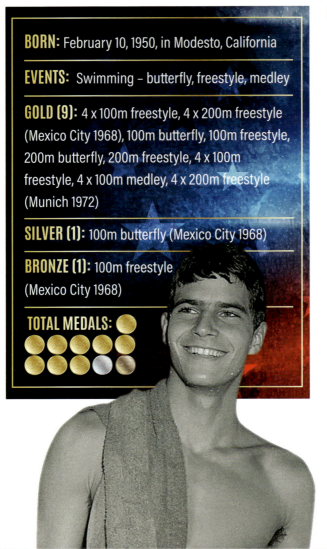

The swimming legend dubbed "Mark the Shark" twice headed off to a Summer Olympics promising to return home with six golds. Spitz, born in California, spent his childhood swimming daily in the sea off Waikiki beach after his family moved to Hawaii when he was two and then with a club in Sacramento when they returned to California four years later. He was already setting age-group records by the time he was ten. Spitz came back from the Mexico City Olympics in 1968, aged 18, with "only" two golds – in the 4 x 100m and 4 x 200m freestyle relays, as well as 100m butterfly silver and 100m freestyle bronze. But he bettered his own repeat prediction four years later in Munich, where he became the first person to complete a haul of seven golds from one Summer Games. His record stood until fellow US swimmer Michael Phelps took eight in Beijing 36 years later. Spitz's seven 1972 triumphs also set records, including four individual races in the 100m and 200m freestyle and 100m and 200m butterfly. Spitz left the Games early, after completing his events, amid concerns for his safety – being Jewish – after the "Munich Massacre" which saw 11 Israeli athletes taken hostage and murdered by terrorists. He retired after Munich and went into the property business but did attempt a comeback 20 years later. Then 41, he failed to make it through US qualification trials for the 1992 Olympics in Barcelona.

JENNY THOMPSON

BORN: February 26, 1973, in Danvers, Massachusetts

EVENTS: Swimming – butterfly, freestyle, medley

GOLD (8): 4 x 100m freestyle, 4 x 100m medley (Barcelona 1992), 4 x 100m freestyle, 4 x 200m freestyle, 4 x 100m medley (Atlanta 1996), 4 x 100m freestyle, 4 x 200m freestyle, 4 x 100m medley (Sydney 2000)

SILVER (3): 100m freestyle (Barcelona 1992) 4 x 100m freestyle, 4 x 100m medley (Athens 2004)

BRONZE (1): 100m freestyle (Sydney 2000)

TOTAL MEDALS:

No American woman has won more Olympic medals than Jenny Thompson, who claimed 12 across four separate Summer Games. All eight of her golds were in relay races, though she did add individual freestyle 100m silver at Barcelona 1992 and bronze in the same event in Sydney eight years later. Thompson's first gold came when she swam the fourth leg of the 4 x 100m freestyle final in Barcelona in a world record time of 54.01, allowing the USA team to overtake China at the last and win in 3:39.46 – another world record. She struggled during US qualification trials for the 1996 Summer Games in Atlanta and missed out on competing there in any individual races, though did win three relay golds. Thompson

DARA TORRES

Only Natalie Coughlin and Jenny Thompson, among American women, can match Dara Torres's array of 12 Olympics swimming medals. Torres won hers across a US record five different Summer Games, between 1984 in Los Angeles and 2008 in Beijing, only sitting out the 2004 event in Athens. She won three of her four silvers in Beijing, where at 41 she became the oldest ever swimmer at an Olympics – and just missed out on gold in the 50m freestyle by a mere 0.01 seconds to Germany's Britta Steffen who finished in 24.06. She did at least become the oldest swimmer to win an Olympics medal, beating the record held by Great Britain's William Robinson who was 38 when claiming men's 200m breaststroke silver at the 1908 Games in London. Australia's Cate Campbell, who finished third in that Beijing race, was just 16 and was born eight years after Torres clinched her first Olympic gold. That was back in 1984 in Los Angeles, where she, Nancy Hogshead, Jenna Johnson and Carrie Steinseifer swam to victory in the 4 x 100m freestyle final. Torres actually tried to compete at a sixth Olympics, targeting the London 2012 event where she would have been 45, but only finished fourth in US trials for the 50m freestyle – with only the top two qualifying.

BORN: April 15, 1967, in Beverly Hills, California

EVENTS: Swimming – butterfly, freestyle, medley

GOLD (4): 4 x 100m freestyle (Los Angeles 1984), 4 x 100m freestyle (Barcelona 1992), 4 x 100m freestyle, 4 x 100m medley (Sydney 2000)

SILVER (4): 4 x 100m medley (Seoul 1988), 50m freestyle, 4 x 100m freestyle, 4 x 100m medley (Beijing 2008)

BRONZE (4): 4 x 100m freestyle (Seoul 1988), 50m freestyle, 100m freestyle, 100m butterfly (Sydney 2000)

TOTAL MEDALS:

retired from swimming after Sydney to concentrate on her studies at medical school before making a comeback – winning five gold medals at the 2002 Pan Pacific Swimming Championships in the Japanese city of Yokohama. She then signed off with two relay silvers at the 2004 Olympics in Athens, where at 31 she was the oldest member of the USA's aquatics team. Thompson, who went on to work as an anesthesiologist, has said: "When I show little kids at clinics my gold medals, no one asks if it was relay or individual – a gold medal is a gold medal, and I have eight."

RIGHT: Jenny Thompson in action during the Women's 100m Butterfly heat at the 2020 Sydney Olympics

AMY VAN DYKEN

A doctor advised Amy Van Dyken as a child to take up swimming to help strengthen her lungs, as she struggled with severe asthma. She went on to become the first American woman in any sport to win four gold medals at one Olympic Games, in Atlanta in 1996 – adding another two in the pool four years later in Sydney, despite being troubled by a shoulder injury. Van Dyken's historic fourth gold at the Atlanta Games was in the 50m freestyle, when she overtook world record-holder Le Jingyi with her final stroke and won in 24.87 to Le's 24.90. Her other individual gold that summer had been even closer, when her 59.13 in the 100m butterfly was just one-hundredth of a second faster than China's Liu Limin. Van Dyken had attempted to intimidate Le by staring at her in the run-up to their race and was criticised four years later for spitting pool water into Inge de Bruijn's lane ahead of their 50m freestyle final – but the Dutch swimmer won, with Van Dyken fourth. After retiring from swimming after Sydney, she took up triathlons while also working as an NFL reporter and radio DJ alongside charity fundraising. She was left paralysed from the waist down after a quad bike accident which severed her spinal cord in June 2014.

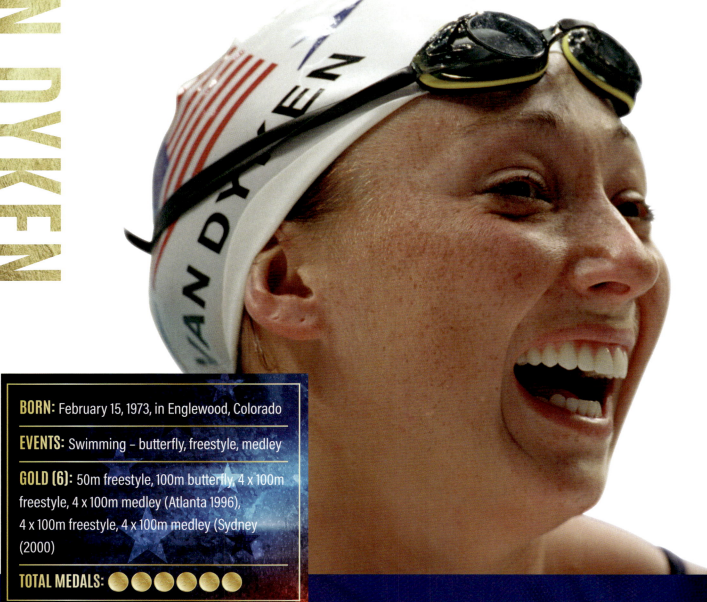

BORN: February 15, 1973, in Englewood, Colorado

EVENTS: Swimming – butterfly, freestyle, medley

GOLD (6): 50m freestyle, 100m butterfly, 4 x 100m freestyle, 4 x 100m medley (Atlanta 1996), 4 x 100m freestyle, 4 x 100m medley (Sydney (2000)

TOTAL MEDALS: 🥇🥇🥇🥇🥇🥇

JOHNNY WEISSMULLER

Johnny Weissmuller might be best known to many for playing Tarzan on the big screen, but he first came to fame for his feats in the water rather than in the film-set jungle. Weissmuller was born in 1904 in Freidorf in what was then in the Kingdom of Hungary and now in Romania. The following year his parents Peter and Elizabeth took him with them to the US, where they first stayed with family in Windber, Pennsylvania, before heading in 1908 to Chicago where Johnny began swimming and quickly established himself as a major talent. In July 1922 he became the first person to swim 100m in less than a minute, 58.6 seconds, and in February 1924 broke his own world record by completing the distance in 57.4. Later that year he won his first three Olympic golds in Paris – as well as helping the USA team to bronze in water polo, beating Sweden 3-2 in a medal play-off. He also entertained locals with a comedy diving act between races. Weissmuller retained his 100m freestyle title four years later in Amsterdam, despite almost passing out after accidentally swallowing too much water, and again anchored the US team's 4 x 200m success. He began training for the 1932 Games in Los Angeles but instead accepted an offer to advertise swimsuits for the BVD Underwear Company before impressing movie scouts in Hollywood who gave him the starring role in "Tarzan, the Ape Man" – the first of his 12 Tarzan films. He originated the famous "Tarzan yell", while beating his chest with his fist, and – at Weissmuller's request – the sound was played three times as his coffin was lowered into the grave after his death in Acapulco, Mexico, aged 79 in January 1984.

BELOW: Poster for the 1928 Summer Olympics in Amsterdam

BORN: June 2, 1904, in Freidorf in what was then the Kingdom of Hungary, now Romania

DIED: January 20, 1984, aged 79, in Acapulco, Mexico

EVENTS: Swimming - freestyle, water polo

GOLD (5): 100m freestyle, 400m freestyle, 4 x 200m freestyle (Paris 1924), 100m freestyle, 4 x 200m freestyle (Amsterdam 1928)

BRONZE (1): Team water polo (Paris 1924)

TOTAL MEDALS: ●●●●●●

BASKETBALL

The United States won the first Olympics basketball gold in 1936, the country's men beating Canada 19-8 in the final, and the country has dominated the event since – with the US men winning 16 of their 19 tournaments and the nation's women eight of their ten. Women's basketball was only added to the Games at Montreal in 1976. Professional players have been allowed to participate since the 1992 Olympics in Barcelona, which saw the USA's "Dream Team" of NBA superstars claim gold.

CARMELO ANTHONY

After the USA gave the Olympics what became globally known as "The Dream Team" in Barcelona in 1992, cruising to men's basketball gold with a selection of top-level NBA players for the first time, some 16 years later they put together what was dubbed "The Redeem Team". After retaining gold in both Atlanta in 1996 and Sydney four years later, the USA surprisingly slumped to just a bronze medal finish in Athens in 2004, defeated 89-81 by Argentina in their semi-final before saving some face with a 104-96 medal play-off win over Lithuania. Carmelo Anthony, playing the small forward position, was a 20-year-old member of that 2004 squad but has since helped his country win gold at Beijing 2008, London 2012 and Rio 2016. That "Redeem Team" in Beijing gained revenge over Argentina by beating them 101-81 in the semi-final, before clinching gold with a 118-107 victory over Spain – with prolific scorer Anthony contributing 13 of the points. Spain were again beaten in the final in London, this time 107-100. Earlier in that tournament Anthony broke the US record for individual scoring in a single game, providing 37 points in just 14 minutes of playing during a 156-73 victory over Nigeria, ahead of Brazil's 138 against Egypt in 1988. The US score that day set a new Olympic record for a single game. Four years later in Rio, Anthony became the first US basketball player to win three golds, as Serbia were defeated 96-66 in the final. The highest single-game scoring of the tournament again came from Anthony, 31 in his side's 98-88 opening round win against Australia.

BORN: May 29, 1984, in New York City, New York

EVENT: Basketball

GOLD (3): Beijing 2008, London 2012, Rio 2016

BRONZE (1): Athens 2004

TOTAL MEDALS:

BASKETBALL

CHARLES BARKLEY

Charles Barkley finished the Barcelona 1992 men's basketball tournament with the USA's top scoring as their "Dream Team" easily while dazzlingly spun their way to gold medal glory. Their triumph was hardly unexpected – this was the first time elite stars from the dominant NBA were allowed to take part in the Olympics. The international Amateur Basketball Federation voted 56-13 in favour of the move, in April 1989 – despite the US being among those voting against changing the amateurs-only rule, fearing for the potential impact on lower-level basketball. But fans – and even awestruck opponents – were dazzled by the talents of players such as Larry Bird, Earvin "Magic" Johnson and Michael Jordan. Their team-mate Barkley played as a power forward but was prized for his versatility, both in attack and defensive, as well as aggressiveness and agility despite the 1.93-tall player being both shorter and stockier than most basketball high-achievers. The Dream Team became the first Olympic basketball team to score at least 100 points in each match, averaging a best-ever 117.3 per game – and beat Croatia 117-85 to secure gold, with Barkley averaging 18 per match. Barkley – nicknamed "Sir Charles" and "The Round Mound of Rebound" – was top scorer in the final four years later, contributing 24 points as the USA retained gold in Atlanta by defeating Yugoslavia 95-69.

TOP LEFT: Barcelona 1992 Olympic Games - one of the official posters

BORN: February 20, 1963, in Leeds, Alabama

EVENT: Basketball

GOLD (2): Barcelona 1992, Atlanta 1996

TOTAL MEDALS: 🥇🥇

OLYMPIC LEGENDS USA

LARRY BIRD

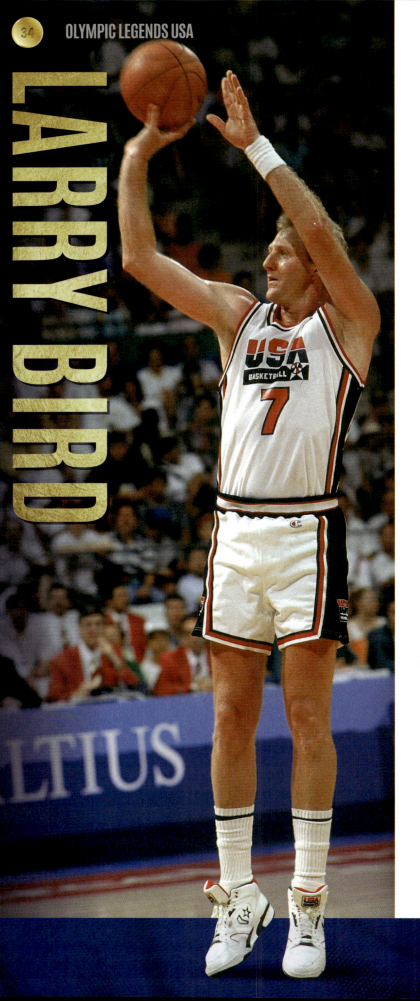

Larry Bird was suffering from back problems and the veteran of the line-up when he and Michael Jordan were chosen as captains of the Barcelona 1992 Summer Olympics "Dream Team". At 35, he was three years older than the next in seniority, 32-year-old Earvin "Magic" Johnson. Yet Bird later described hearing the US national anthem, "The Star-Spangled Banner", when they were ultimately awarded their gold medals as "the ultimate experience". This was the first time NBA basketball players were permitted to compete at the Games. Boston Celtics star Bird, adept at playing either small forward or power forward, top-scored with 19 points when the USA beat Germany 111-68 in the opening round in Barcelona. Away from the Olympics, the man nicknamed "The Hick from French Lick" for his humble origins in a small town in Indiana was a three-time NBA champion as a player before going on to be named NBA Coach of the Year in 1998 and NBA Executive of the Year in 2012. His career-long rivalry with his friend Johnson started when they faced each other in college basketball, Bird for Indiana State and Johnson for Michigan State in a 1979 championship game won by Johnson's side.

LEFT: Larry Bird shoots versus Angola during Men's Group A game at the 1992 Summer Olympics

BORN: December 7, 1956, in West Baden Springs, Indiana

EVENT: Basketball

GOLD (1): Barcelona 1992

TOTAL MEDALS: 🥇

BASKETBALL

SUE BIRD

Sue Bird went into the 2020 Olympics in Tokyo, delayed until the following year due to the Covid 19-pandemic, carrying the US flag at the opening ceremony on July 3, 2021. She ended the summer with a record fifth gold medal for women's basketball, helping her country win the event for the seventh consecutive Summer Games. Four-time WBNA champion Bird ended the 2020 tournament with the US side's best record for assists, an average of 6.5 per game, with the team beating Japan 90-75 in the final. The win took her past the four basketball golds won by Teresa Edwards and by Lisa Leslie, who had been Bird's team-mate during the Athens 2004 and Beijing 2008 triumphs. The last time anyone other than the US won women's basketball Olympic gold was when a post-USSR Unified Team beat the US 79-73 in the semis and then China 76-66 in the final. Point guard Bird spent 20 years with WBNA side the Seattle Storm after first being drafted in 2000 and their 2020 title triumph made her the first person to win the WBNA championship in three different decades. She announced her retirement at the age of 41 in June 2022.

LEFT: One of the posters from the 2000 Sydney Olympic Games

BORN: October 16, 1980, in Syosset, New York

EVENT: Basketball

GOLD (5): Athens 2004, Beijing 2008, London 2012, Rio 2016, Tokyo 2020

TOTAL MEDALS: 🥇🥇🥇🥇🥇

KOBE BRYANT

Los Angeles Lakers favourite Kobe Bryant had just been named NBA's Most Valuable Player when he helped the USA regain their Olympic title in Beijing in 2008, four years after a disappointing bronze in Athens. This time they reached the final where they faced Spain, whose main man was Bryant's Lakers team-mate Pau Gasol – top scorer at the 2004 Olympics. The Americans' lead was just four points with only a little over two minutes of the final left, but three-pointers by Dwayne Wade and Bryant completed a 118-107 triumph for the US. Shooting guard Bryant scored 20 points that day, averaging 15 across the tournament – and the climax of the final against Spain was typical of his fondness for trying shots in the final moments of a closely-fought game, no matter how unlikely they looked. He was there again on the winners' podium four years later in London, after scoring 20 in the 119-86 quarter-final victory over Australia, 13 to help beat Argentina 109-83 in the semi and another 17 as Gasol and Spain were again seen off in the final, albeit only narrowly in a 107-100 finish. Bryant died aged 41 in January 2020 when a helicopter carrying him crashed into the side of a mountain in Calabasas, California. Also killed were his 13-year-old daughter Gianna, six of his friends and the pilot Ara Zobayan.

BORN: August 23, 1978, in Philadelphia, Pennsylvania

DIED: January 26, 2020, aged 41, in Calabasas, California

EVENT: Basketball

GOLD (2): Beijing 2008, London 2012

TOTAL MEDALS: ●●

TERESA EDWARDS

Teresa Edwards was a member of the squad which took women's basketball Olympic gold for the first time in Los Angeles in 1984, after the Soviet Union triumphed the only two previous events in Montreal in 1976 and Moscow in 1980. She was still winning in 2000 in Sydney, this time collecting a record fourth basketball gold. She holds the records for both youngest women's basketball gold medallist, aged 20 in 1984 and 36 in 2000. In between there were further golds in Atlanta in 1996 and Sydney four years later, after the relative disappointment of bronze at Barcelona in 1992 where the USA lost their semi-final 79-73 to Russia. Edwards and her team-mates clinched their first gold by defeating South Korea 85-55 in the 1984 final, then four years later retained gold with a 77-70 victory over Yugoslavia as Edwards averaged 16 points per game for the tournament and was the USA's top scorer in three of their five fixtures. Brazil were beaten 111-87 in the final Atlanta showdown, before Edwards bowed out in Sydney with a fourth gold thanks to defeating the hosts Australia 76-54. She took a moment sitting alone in the centre of the court to mark her triumphant Olympics farewell. After playing college basketball as a starting point guard for the Georgia Lady Bulldogs while at the University of Georgia – she was a student there when winning her first Olympic gold – Edwards went on to play for the Minnesota Lynx in the WBNA as well as for teams overseas in France, Japan, Italy and Spain.

LEBRON JAMES

LeBron James helped spearhead the second wave of NBA stars propelling the USA back to Olympic glory after their surprise bronze at Athens 2004. The pacy and strong player also admired for his passing skills was part of that 2004 side though spent most of the tournament on the bench, later describing the experience as a "lowlight". But he proved key when the country returned to gold medal-winning ways in Beijing four years later, personally contributing 14 points, six rebounds and three assists as the USA beat Spain 118-107 in the final. He took more responsibility from older team-mate Kobe Bryant at London 2012 as the USA retained their title, leading the attack and his 19 points in the final – again beating Spain – made him the USA's all-time leading international scorer. James has been at the centre of controversies during his playing career, including the circumstances surrounding his departure from his hometown NBA side the Cleveland Cavaliers in 2010. He announced which club he would join, the Miami Heat, in a nationwide live TV programme called The Decision which raised millions of dollars for charity but upset Cavaliers fans as well as rival clubs hoping to sign him. He rejoined his former club four years later before moving to the Los Angeles Lakers in 2018.

BORN: December 30, 1984, in Akron, Ohio
EVENT: Basketball
GOLD (2): Beijing 2008, London 2012
TOTAL MEDALS: 🥇🥇

BORN: July 19, 1964, in Cairo, Georgia
EVENT: Basketball
GOLD (4): Los Angeles 1984, Seoul 1988, Atlanta 1996, Sydney 2000
BRONZE (1): Barcelona 1992
TOTAL MEDALS: 🥇🥇🥇🥇🥉

"MAGIC" JOHNSON

BORN: August 14, 1959, in Lansing, Michigan
EVENT: Basketball
GOLD (1): Barcelona 1992
TOTAL MEDALS: 🥇

When the US sent their spectacular "Dream Team" of NBA stars to the Olympics for the first time in 1992, in Barcelona, coach Chuck Daly described the excited fervour surrounding them as "like Elvis and The Beatles" put together. At the heart of this was point guard and co-captain Earvin "Magic" Johnson, in many people's minds the greatest basketball player ever. He had retired from the sport in 1991, after being diagnosed as HIV-positive. The five-time NBA champion and three-time NBA Most Valuable Player missed two matches in Barcelona due to knee problems but started five of the other six, averaging – and later called that Olympics summer "the greatest moment of my life in terms of basketball, bar none". He had first got his nickname "Magic" as a 15-year-old at Everett High School in Michigan, after achieving a so-called "triple-double" – ten or more in three different categories, in one game – with 36 points, 18 rebounds and 16 assists. He spent his top-level playing career with the Los Angeles Lakers, between 1979 and 1991 as well as a brief comeback in 1996. After his final retirement, he ran the Magic Johnson Foundation which had been set up initially to help tackle HIV and Aids and now also supports educational, health and social causes.

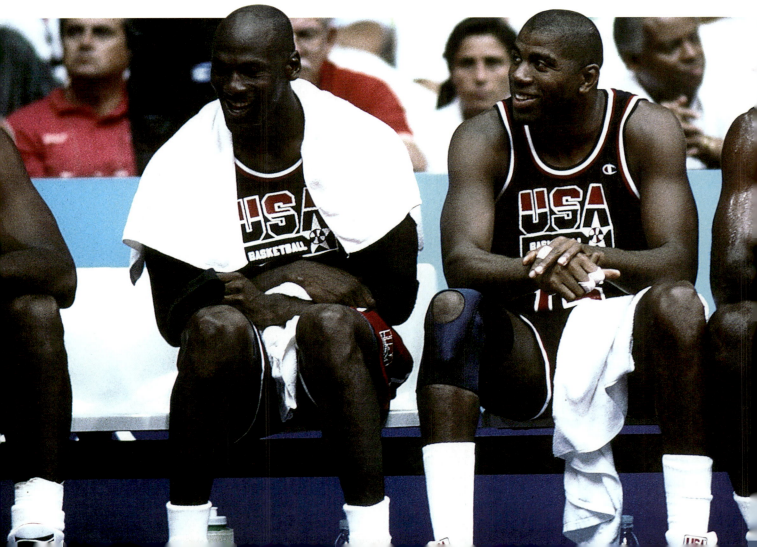

BELOW: Michael Jordan (L) and Magic Johnson (R) sit on the bench during the 1992 Summer Olympics in Barcelona

BASKETBALL

MICHAEL JORDAN

BORN: February 17, 1963, in New York, New York City
EVENT: Basketball
GOLD (2): Los Angeles 1984, Barcelona 1992
TOTAL MEDALS: 🥇🥇

The man described by the NBA as "the greatest basketball player of all time" was also the only member of the 1992 "Dream Team" who went into the Games in Barcelona having already won Olympic gold. The shooting guard and slam dunk specialist averaged 17.1 points per game as the US side won all eight games at the 1984 Olympics in Los Angeles, beating Spain 96-65 in the final. Chicago Bulls star and six-time NBA champion Jordan was offered the role of "Dream Team" captain by head coach Chuck Daly ahead of the 1992 Games but turned it down, with Larry Bird and Earvin "Magic" Johnson given the roles instead. But Jordan did start all eight matches in Barcelona, averaging 14.9 points per game – second only to Charles Barkley's 18. Jordan is also said to have been the only member of the team who studied their opponents in advance, despite how comfortable the victories would all prove. Jordan's spectacular technique, all-round attacking and defensive game and consistency helped hugely boost basketball's appeal, both with fans and sponsors. He became one of the world's most famous sportsmen and his "Air Jordan" nickname – inspired by his leaping abilities – was given to a range of bestselling trainers by the sportswear giant Nike. He also starred alongside Looney Tunes cartoon characters such as Bugs Bunny, Daffy Duck and Porky Pig in the 1996 movie Space Jam.

LISA LESLIE

BORN: July 7, 1972, in Compton, California
EVENT: Basketball
GOLD (4): Atlanta 1996, Sydney 2000, Athens 2004, Beijing 2008
TOTAL MEDALS: 🥇🥇🥇🥇

The US women's basketball team has won the last seven Olympic golds, a run that began with glory at the 1996 Games in Atlanta where their stars included prolific center Lisa Leslie. The 1.96m-tall player top-scored in the quarter-final, semi-final and final – respectively contributing an Olympic and US record record 35 points when Japan were beaten 108-93, then 22 in a 93-71 victory over Australia and culminating with another 29 to help see off Brazil 111-87. That gave Leslie the first of four Olympic gold medals, her last coming when reigning world champions Australia were beaten 92-65 in the Beijing 2008 final. That was the third Olympics in a row where Leslie and the US won gold against Australia, whose star player Lauren Jackson had a long-running rivalry with Leslie – intensified when Jackson pulled off Leslie's hair extension during the Sydney 2000 final which the US won 76-54. Leslie and her team-mates retained the title against the same opponents four years later in Athens, 74-63, with Leslie contributing eight rebounds. Leslie, who played for the Los Angeles Sparks from the WBNA's start in 1997 until her retirement in 2009, still holds the US women's international basketball records for most points (488), rebounds (241) and blocks (37).

BOXING

The United States has topped the boxing medals table since its introduction at the 1904 Olympics in St Louis, with 117 overall medals including 50 golds – well ahead of second-placed Cuba's 78. The only Games where the sport was missing was in Stockholm in 1912, because the Swedish government banned boxing at the time. The 2024 Paris Olympics will have the men competing in seven different weight divisions and the women in six. Women's boxing was only added as an Olympic sport at London 2012 and until 2016 Olympic boxing was for amateur or state-funded competitors only.

CASSIUS CLAY

The boxer later to become Muhammad Ali and self-styled "The Greatest" burst into the spotlight by winning Olympic gold as an 18-year-old light heavyweight in Rome in 1960. His amateur career, which began in 1954, included 100 wins and five defeats – culminating in his victory over Poland's three-time European champion Zbigniew Pietrzykowski in the Rome final on a unanimous decision. Clay, who changed his name to Muhammad Ali in March 1964, made his professional heavyweight boxing debut in October 1960. He was hailed world champion for the first time in February 1964, taking the title from Sonny Liston. Ali was stripped of his boxing license and titles in 1966 after refusing conscription into the US Army to fight in Vietnam, only returning to action in 1970. His so-called "Fight Of The Century" against Joe Frazier at Madison Square Garden in New York in March 1971 brought Ali a first professional defeat, on points, but he gained revenge with a 14th-round win against Frazier in January 1974. That gave him a shot at reigning world heavyweight champion George Foreman in what was billed "The Rumble In The Jungle" in Kinshasa in what was then known as Zaire, now the Democratic Republic of Congo. Ali won the October 1974 bout with an eighth-round knock-out. Ali ended his professional career with a record of 56 wins and five defeats and his death in 2016 prompted worldwide mourning.

TOP RIGHT: Muhammad Ali defeats Soviet boxer Gennady Schatkov to proceed to the next round at the 1960 Olympics in Rome

BORN: January 17, 1942, in Louisville, Kentucky

DIED: June 3, 2016, aged 74, in Scottsdale Arizona

EVENT: Boxing – light heavyweight

GOLD (1): Rome 1960

TOTAL MEDALS:

GEORGE FOREMAN

Future two-time world heavyweight champion George Foreman had only fought 18 matches before going into the 1968 Summer Olympics in Mexico City, but ended the tournament with the gold medal around his neck – having celebrated his final victory by walking around the ring holding aloft a US flag. He was 10 years younger than his opponent, the USSR's Jonas Čepulis, but won in the second round when the referee stopped the fight. Foreman would later say his Olympic triumph meant more to him than his heavyweight championship belts. Foreman's first world title came when knocking out defending champion Joe Frazier in January 1973 in Kingston, Jamaica – but he was knocked down and lost for the first time in the famed "Rumble In The Jungle" against Muhammad Ali in October the following year. He later became a born-again Christian and minister after a health scare in his dressing room following defeat to Jimmy Young in 1977, but returned to the ring ten years later partly to raise money for a youth centre he set up. He shocked many by knocking out Michael Moorer in November 1995 to regain the world heavyweight boxing crown and become, at 45, the oldest fighter to win a world championship.

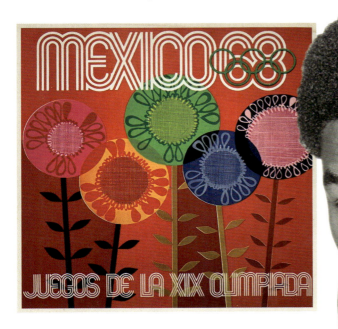

ABOVE: One of many official posters from the Mexico Olympics 1968

Born: January 10, 1949, in Marshall, Texas

Event: Boxing – heavyweight

Gold (1): Mexico City 1968

Total medals:

JOE FRAZIER

Joe Frazier went to the 1964 Summer Olympics only as a late stand-in after the US's first-choice contender Buster Mathis broke a knuckle – Mathis had previously inflicted the only two defeats of Frazier's 40-match amateur career. The heavyweight fighter who would later be widely known as "Smokin' Joe" knocked out Uganda's George Oywello in the round of 16, then Australia's Athol McQueen after just 40 seconds of their quarter-final. He reached the final when Vadim Yemelyanov of the USSR conceded in the second round but victory came at a cost – Frazier broke the thumb of his favoured and pummelling left hand when delivering the final blow. Yet he kept his injury secret, used his right hand more than normal in the final against Germany's Hans Huber and won the decision 3-2. Frazier, 20 at the time, was the USA's only boxing Olympic champion that year. After going professional in 1965, he became undisputed world heavyweight boxing champion in 1970 and in February the following year inflicted Muhammad Ali's first professional defeat in a unanimous decision after what was dubbed the "Fight Of The Century". Despite years of enmity between the pair, Ali was among those attending and applauding at Frazier's 2011 funeral in Philadelphia after his death from liver cancer at the age of 67.

BORN: January 12, 1944, in Beaufort, South Carolina

DIED: November 7, 2011, aged 67, in Philadelphia, Pennsylvania

EVENT: Boxing – heavyweight

GOLD (1): Tokyo 1964

TOTAL MEDALS:

OSCAR DE LA HOYA

Oscar De La Hoya was devastated when his mother Cecilia was diagnosed terminally ill with breast cancer in 1990. Before 38-year-old Cecilia's death in October that year he promised her he would win Olympic boxing gold – and did so in Barcelona in 1992, stopping Germany's Marco Rudolph in the third round of their final. De La Hoya, 20, had knelt in the ring and pointed to the sky in honour of his late mother after winning his first bouts at the Games and marked his final victory by carrying not only a US flag but also a Mexican one – Cecilia and his father Joel, a professional boxer himself, had moved across the border from Mexico before Oscar was born. He also took his gold medal to her grave on returning to his Los Angeles home. De La Hoya's Olympic success led to him being labelled "The Golden Boy" and his move into the professional ranks would see him win world lightweight, super lightweight, welterweight, light middleweight and middleweight titles. He was also nominated for a Grammy for his 2000 Latin pop album Oscar De La Hoya, featuring music written by international chart-toppers the Bee Gees.

BORN: February 4, 1973, in East Los Angeles, California

EVENT: Boxing - lightweight

GOLD (1): Barcelona 1992

TOTAL MEDALS: 🥇

ABOVE: Pictured here in 1998 as the WBC welterweight champion, Oscar De La Hoya had built on his Olympic success to become a multi-weight world champion in the pro ranks

EDDIE EAGAN

Eddie Eagan won two Olympic gold medals – one Summer, one Winter. His first came at the 1920 Summer Games in Antwerp, where he defeated Norway's Sverre Sørsdal in the final. He failed to win a medal after moving into the heavyweight division four years later in Paris, but returned to Olympic action in 1932 – this time at the Winter Games at Lake Placid, where he was part of the USA's triumphant four-man bobsleigh team. This made him the first – and so far only – person to win Summer and Winter Olympics golds in different disciplines. Sweden's Gillis Grafström won figure skating gold at the Antwerp 1920 Summer Olympics and at the Chamonix 1924 and St Moritz 1928 Winter Olympics. Eagan's other sporting successes included winning the Amateur Athletic Union's heavyweight boxing crown in 1919 and the Amateur Boxing Association's four years later. He also worked as a lawyer after studying at Yale University, Harvard Law School and Oxford University.

"SUGAR" RAY LEONARD

Ray Charles Leonard – named after his mother Getha's favourite singer – gained his nickname after US Olympic boxing team assistant coach Sarge Johnson told colleague Dave Jacobs: "That kid you got is sweet as sugar." Leonard competed in US Olympic trials ahead of the 1972 Summer Olympics in Munich despite being only 16, a year younger than allowed, but lost in the lightweight semi-finals. He did make the team for the 1976 Games in Montreal, however, where he won gold after six consecutive 5-0 decisions – the final one against Cuba's Andrés Aldama. Leonard boxed that summer wearing pictures of future wife Juanita Wilkinson and their two-year-old son Ray Charles Leonard Jr taped to his sock. He initially announced after victory that he would be quitting boxing but changed his mind and went professional, embarking on a career which brought welterweight, light middleweight, middleweight, super middleweight and light heavyweight world championships. He was dubbed one of the so-called "Four Kings" of boxing in the 1980s, compelling attention with epic bouts against Panama's Roberto Durán and fellow Americans Thomas Hearns and Marvin Hagler. Another boxer nicknamed "Sugar Ray" won Olympic light welterweight gold four years before Leonard did – Ray Seales, also fighting for the US, beat Bulgaria's Angel Angelov in the Munich 1972 final.

ABOVE: Sugar Ray Leonard taking part in the 1976 US Olympic team boxing trials

BORN: May 17, 1956, in Wilmington, North Carolina

EVENT: Boxing – light welterweight

GOLD (1): Montreal 1976

TOTAL MEDALS: 🥇

BORN: April 26, 1897, in Denver, Colorado

DIED: June 14, 1967, aged 70, in New York City, New York

EVENT: Boxing – light heavyweight

GOLD (1): Antwerp 1920

TOTAL MEDALS (INCLUDING 1 WINTER GAMES IN BOBSLEIGH): 🥇🥇

FLOYD PATTERSON

Seventeen-year-old Floyd Patterson needed just 74 seconds to win Olympic middleweight gold in Helsinki in 1952, landing an uppercut to the chin of Romania's Vasile Tiță which secured a first-round knock-out. Patterson's so-called "peek-a-boo" stance became a familiar feature of his approach, holding his hands in front of his face – higher than most boxers would have them. He combined nimble mobility with hefty punching power, but his shy and sensitive manner also contributed to him being known as "The Gentleman of Boxing". He became the first Olympic gold medallist to win a professional heavyweight championship, when he beat fellow American Archie Moore in November 1956. Patterson was just 21 at the time, the youngest man to win the heavyweight championship until 20-year-old Mike Tyson in 1987, and became the first man to regain the heavyweight title when avenging in June 1960 an earlier defeat to Sweden's Ingemar Johansson before beating him again the following March. His final fight, at the age of 37, was a seventh-round defeat to Muhammad Ali in September 1972. He later trained his adopted son Tracy Harris Patterson, who became WBO super bantamweight champion in 1992. Patterson died in May 2006 after suffering from prostate cancer and Alzheimer's disease.

BORN: January 4, 1935, in Waco, North Carolina

DIED: May 11, 2006, aged 71, in New Paltz, New York

EVENTS: Boxing – middleweight

GOLD (1): Helsinki 1952

TOTAL MEDALS: 🥇

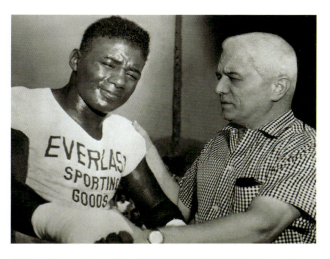

ABOVE: Floyd Patterson with legendary trainer Cus D'Amato

FOOTBALL

Football is the official designation for the sport at the Olympics, rather than soccer. The FIFA World Cup is undisputed as the game's top prize but until its launch in 1930, the Olympics had been seen as an unofficial world championship – with Uruguay winning in 1924 and 1928 ahead of landing that first World Cup as hosts. Since 1992, the Olympics men's tournament has been limited to players aged under 23 except for three over-age players in each squad. No restrictions affect the women's event. The US women have won gold four times, including at the first women's event in 1996, as well as silver in 2000 and bronze at Tokyo 2020, while the men's only medals have been silver in 1904 and bronze four years later.

BRANDI CHASTAIN

Men have been playing association football at the Summer Olympics since the modern Games were held for the second time, in Paris in 1900, but women's football was not added until 1996 in Atlanta. Since then the US have won four of the seven tournaments, including the first – three years before the country became the first to lift the Women's World Cup for a second time. Among the team members playing a key part on both occasions was defender Brandi Chastain, who scored the winning shoot-out penalty against China to secure that 1999 triumph and famously celebrated by removing her shirt to reveal her black sports bra as she slid on her knees and shouted to the skies. She played every minute of the 1996 Olympics tournament, which culminated in a 2-1 victory over China, and started the final in Athens eight years later when the US beat Brazil by the same scoreline. That regained the Olympic title lost in a 3-2 extra-time defeat by Norway in the Sydney 2000 final. Chastain scored 30 goals in 192 international appearances between 1988 and 2004.

BORN: July 21, 1968, in San Jose, California

EVENT: Football

POSITION: Defender, midfielder

GOLD (2): Atlanta 1996, Athens 2004

SILVER (1): Sydney 2000

TOTAL MEDALS: 🥇🥇🥈

MIA HAMM

One of the world's all-time greatest women's footballers, Mia Hamm captained the US team at their first three Olympics – leading them to gold at Atlanta 1996 and Athens 2004, while just falling short in the Sydney final in between. Despite being born with a club foot, Hamm was already playing for a team at the age of five after falling in love with football while living with her family in Florence, in soccer-mad Italy. She made her international debut aged just 15 in 1987, helped the US win the first FIFA Women's World Cup in 1991 when beating Norway in the final then scored in their first Olympics match in 1996 – a 3-0 preliminary round win over Denmark. She struggled with foot and groin injuries throughout the tournament but was an inspirational presence en route to gold – even though she needed to be stretchered off in the closing moments of the final, having set up Shannon MacMillan's opener in the 2-1 win over China. She scored what was then a record 127th international goal – for men or women – to put the US into the 2000 Olympics final at the expense of Brazil, before a 3-2 loss to Norway, but after leading her team to gold again in Athens four years later she was chosen to carry the US flag at that Games' closing ceremony. Only two women have scored more than her 158 international goals, in 276 games.

BELOW: One of the official posters from the 1996 Atlanta Games

BORN: March 17, 1972, in Selma, Alabama

EVENT: Football

POSITION: Forward, midfielder

GOLD (2): Atlanta 1996, Athens 2004

SILVER (1): Sydney 2000

TOTAL MEDALS:

KRISTINE LILLY

Kristine Lilly was another crucial mainstay of the dominant US sides who won the 1991 and 1999 FIFA Women' World Cups and contested the first three Olympics women's football finals – winning gold in 1996 and 2004 either side of 2000 silver. It was Lilly's corner kick which was headed in by striker Abby Wambach eight minutes from the end of extra-time, to beat Brazil 2-1 in the 2004 final. Lilly had opened the scoring in the semi-final only for Germany to equalise three minutes into stoppage-time, before 19-year-old Heather O'Reilly gave the US an extra-time 2-1 win. Lilly scored four Olympics goals, one in 2000 and three four years later. She also claimed the record for international appearances in both the men's or women's game, winning 354 caps in a 23-year career for her country following her US debut in 1987. Her goal against England in September 2007 made her the oldest person to score at a Women's World Cup, aged 36. But she missed the following year's Olympics in Beijing – where the US beat Brazil 1-0 in the gold medal final – having just given birth to first daughter Sidney.

BORN: July 22, 1971, in New York City, New York
EVENT: Football
POSITION: Forward, midfielder
GOLD (2): Atlanta 1996, Athens 2004
SILVER (1): Sydney 2000
TOTAL MEDALS: 🥇🥇🥈

MEGAN RAPINOE

Rosy pink-haired skipper Megan Rapinoe has been one of the most familiar personalities in US sport and women's football in recent years, helping spearhead the national team to triumphs at the London 2012 Summer Olympics and the FIFA Women's World Cup in 2015 and 2019. Her three goals at London 2012 included two equalisers in a 4-3 semi-final victory over Canada, including one directly from a corner. She also set up Carli Lloyd's second goal in the final, clinching a 2-1 win against Japan – midfielder Lloyd had previously scored the only goal of the 2008 final against Brazil. But despite going into the Tokyo 2020 Olympics as reigning world champions, after the 2019 Women's World Cup where Rapinoe won the Golden Boot for top scorer and Golden Ball for Best player, she and her team-mates had to settle for bronze this time. They lost 1-0 to eventual gold medallists Canada in their semi-final, though Rapinoe did sign off with two goals to help beat Australia 4-3 in the bronze medal match. She has been one of the women's game's most prominent performers, internationally and playing on US teams such as Chicago Red Stars, Philadelphia Independence, Seattle Sounders Women and most recently Seattle Reign. Rapinoe has also had successful spells overseas with Sydney FC in Australia and Olympique Lyonnais in France.

BORN: July 5, 1985, in Redding, California
EVENT: Football
POSITION: Midfielder, winger
GOLD (1): London 2012
BRONZE (1): Tokyo 2020
TOTAL MEDALS: 🥇🥉

FOOTBALL

ABBY WAMBACH

As a soccer-mad kid, and highly competitive as the youngest of seven siblings, Abby Wambach would often stay on longer after practice at school to fine-tune her heading abilities. It was her head she used to clinch Olympic gold for the US at the 2004 Olympics in Athens, nodding in a late winner from Kristine Lilly's corner to defeat Brazil 2-1 in the final. Wambach is the US's all-time top international scorer with 184 goals in 256 games, including four strikes at Athens 2004 and another five in London eight years later where she found the net in every match except the final. She scored 27 for her country in the calendar year 2012 alongside strike partner Alex Morgan who hit 28 – equalling a US combined record of 56 set in 1991 by Michelle Akers (39) and Carin Jennings (16), both of whom would go on to win Olympic gold in Atlanta in 1996. Wambach's last Olympic goal was an 80th-minute penalty equaliser to make it 3-3 against Canada in their London 2012 semi-final, played at Manchester United's Old Trafford stadium in northern England. Morgan headed the winner to make it 4-3 to the US, three minutes into extra-time stoppage-time.

BORN: June 2, 1980, in Rochester, New York
EVENT: Football
POSITION: Forward
GOLD (2): Athens 2004, London 2012
TOTAL MEDALS:

BELOW: 2012 London Olympic Games poster

GOLF

Golf was played at the 1900 Olympics in Paris and in St Louis four years later, but there was then an 112-year absence before the sport returned at the 2016 Games in Rio. The United States tops the overall medal table with 15, (5 golds) – including a double US triumph of Xander Schauffele and Nelly Korda at Tokyo 2020. A men's team event was held at the 1904 Olympics but otherwise there have only been men's individual and women's individual tournaments.

MARGARET ABBOTT

Margaret Abbott was the first American woman to become an Olympic champion – although she never knew it. The Chicago socialite had travelled to Paris with mother Mary in 1899 to study art then signed up for a women's golf tournament the following year, unaware it was part of the second modern-day Olympic Games. She won the 10-woman event with a score of 47 strokes, receiving a porcelain bowl as a prize, while her mother finished seventh. Women were allowed to take part in only five sports in that summer's Olympics – as well as golf, they competed in equestrianism, rowing, sailing and tennis. The US also provided what would have been silver and bronze medallists behind Abbott – Pauline "Polly" Whittier runner-up with 49 shots and Daria Pratt finishing with a further four. Abbott's son Philip Dunne, later an Oscar-nominated screenplay writer and director, said his mother attributed her success to French rivals turning up to play "in high heels and skirts". Abbott died five days before her 77th birthday in June 1955, still oblivious to being an Olympic champion – a fact which was only discovered by Olympic Board of Directors member Paula Welch while researching her life in the 1970s.

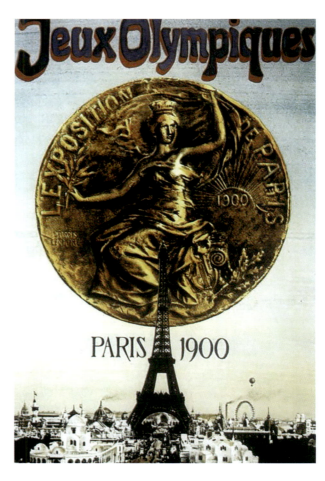

ABOVE: One of the official posters of the 1900 Paris Summer Olympics

RIGHT: Margaret Abbott plays in the 1900 Olympic Games women's golf event in Compiègne, France

BORN: June 15, 1878, in what was Calcutta, now Kolkata, in what was British India, now India

DIED: June 10, 1955, in Greenwich, Connecticut

EVENT: Golf

GOLD (1): Paris 1900

TOTAL MEDALS: 🥇

NELLY KORDA

GOLF

Women's golf was restored to the Summer Olympics at Rio 2016, 116 years after its previous inclusion at Paris 1900. South Korea's Inbee Park took gold in Rio, Lydia Ko of New Zealand won silver and China's Shanshan Feng bronze. The US had to wait another five years for their first female Olympic champion since Margaret Abbott, when Nelly Korda triumphed at the Covid-19 pandemic-delayed Tokyo Games in August 2021. It came two months after she won her first major, the 2021 Women's PGA Championship. Korda secured Olympic gold by hitting rounds of 67, 62, 69 and 69 to finish 17 under par — a stroke clear of Japan's Mone Inami and New Zealand's Ko, with Inami then winning a play-off to take silver. Sporting talent runs in Korda's family — her Czech professional tennis player father Petr Korda won the Australian Open men's singles in 1988 while her elder sister Jessica Korda, a fellow golfer, clinched the Australian Women's Open in 2012. Petr caddied for Nelly when she took part in the 2013 US Women's Open when she was aged just 14.

BORN: July 28, 1998, in Bradenton, Florida
EVENT: Golf
GOLD (1): Tokyo 2020
TOTAL MEDALS:

CHARLES SANDS

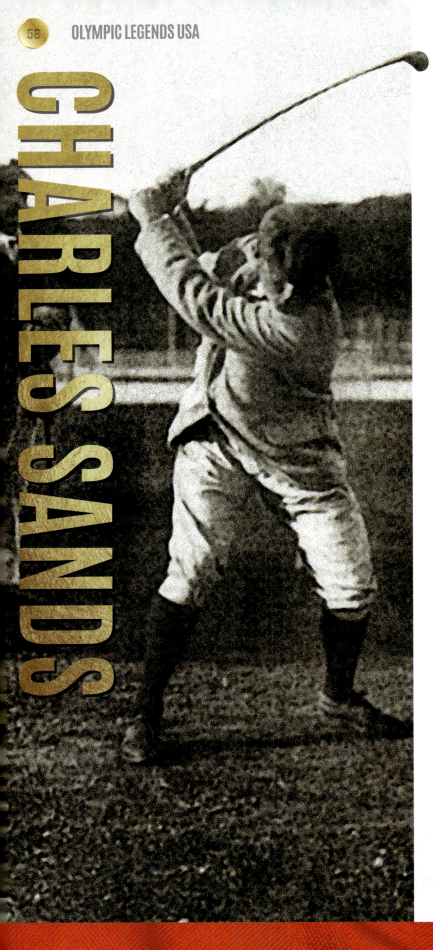

Twelve men from four countries took part in the first men's golf event at an Olympics, at the Compiègne Golf Club as part of the Summer Games in Paris on October 2 1900. After each competitor shot two 18-hole rounds, the US's Charles Sands was crowned winner with a score of 167 strokes – one ahead of Great Britain's Walter Rutherford whose compatriot David Robertson took bronze after finishing on 175. France's two competitors Pierre Deschamps and J. Van de Wynckélé came 10th and 12th respectively, either side of Greece's sole entrant Alexandros Merkati. Sands also took part in the Paris tennis tournament, though lost in the first round three times – in the men's singles to Great Britain's Harold Mahony; in the men's doubles, alongside Great Britain's Archibald Warden, to eventual silver medallists Spalding de Garmendia of the US and France's Max Decugis, and in the mixed doubles with fellow American Georginia Jones, to compatriot Marion Jones and Great Britain's Laurie Doherty. Sands returned to the Olympics eight years later in London, but suffered another first round exit in the real tennis – also called "jeu de paume" – when beaten by Great Britain's Eustace Miles.

LEFT: Charles Sands tees off during the 1900 Olympic Games in Paris

BORN: December 22, 1865, in New York

DIED: August 9, 1945, aged 79, in Brookville, New York

EVENT: Golf

GOLD (1): Paris 1900

TOTAL MEDALS:

XANDER SCHAUFFELE

GOLF

US teams took gold, silver and bronze at the 1904 Olympics in St Louis – a Western Golf Association selection coming first, the Trans Mississippi Golf Association second and the United States Golf Association third. That was the last of golf as an Olympic sport until Rio 2016, when in the men's event Great Britain's Justin Rose won gold, Henrik Stenson of Sweden silver and the US's best effort came from bronze medallist Matt Kuchar. Xander Schauffele clinched gold for the US at Tokyo 2020, shooting rounds of 68, 63, 68 and 67 to finish 18 under par on 266 – one ahead of silver-winning Rory Sabbatini of Slovakia, before Chinese Taipei's Pan Cheng-tsung prevailed in a bronze medal play-off after finishing level with six others on 269. Schauffele's mother was raised in Japan and he had grandparents living in Tokyo but they were unable to attend the event due to Covid-19 restrictions on spectators at live events. Sabbatani finished his final round in an Olympic record low of 61 strokes, but Schauffele's 4ft par putt secured a narrow and tense win. Away from the Olympics, Schauffele's best performances at majors were tied second places at the 2018 Open Championships and the Masters the following year – though the month after his Olympic triumph he helped the US beat Europe in the 2021 Ryder Cup.

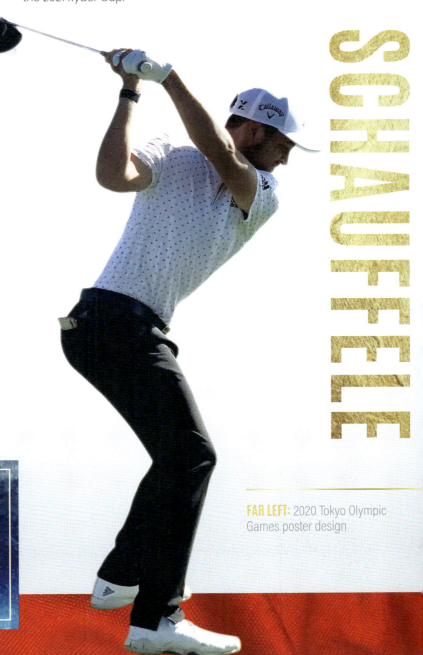

FAR LEFT: 2020 Tokyo Olympic Games poster design

BORN: October 25, 1993, in San Diego, California

EVENT: Golf

GOLD (1): Tokyo 2020

TOTAL MEDALS: 🥇

GYMNASTICS

Olympic gymnastics has three disciplines: artistic, rhythmic and trampoline. Artistic events see gymnasts judged on how they perform on a series of apparatus, while rhythmic – for female competitors only – involves graceful movements to music holding different implements and trampolinists are marked for their skills on those sprung surfaces. Gymnastics has played a part at every Olympics since Athens 1896, initially for men only until women's events were added in Amsterdam in 1928.

SIMONE BILES

Simone Biles was one of the stand-out – while somersaulting – sensations of the Rio 2016 Summer Olympics, which ended with her becoming the first female gymnast given the honour of carrying the US flag at the Closing Ceremony. By that point she had become the first woman to win four artistic gymnastics golds at a single Summer Games since Romania's Ecaterina Szabo in Los Angeles in 1984 and only the fifth in history. Biles's first was in the all-around team event, where she was the only US gymnast to perform in all events in the final. She followed this triumph with individual golds in the all-around, vault and floor exercise finals and bronze in the vault. She reached all individual finals at Tokyo 2020 but pulled out of the team competition amid mental health struggles – only returning for the beam final, where she won bronze with a scaled-back routine of less complexity than her usual spectacular performances. Biles later explained she had been suffering "the twisties", a psychological state depriving her of the usual air awareness while carrying out twists. Simone has been praised for speaking publicly about mental health as well as how she has been diagnosed with attention deficit hyperactivity disorder. Biles and her three siblings spent time in foster care as children before she and younger sister Adria were formally adopted in 2003 by her maternal grandfather Ron Biles and his second wife Nellie Cayetano Biles. US president Joe Biden awarded her the Presidential Medal of Freedom in July 2022, making then-25-year-old Biles the youngest person to receive the country's highest civilian honour.

BORN: March 14, 1997, in Columbus, Ohio

EVENT: Artistic gymnastics

GOLD (4): Team all-around, individual all-around, vault, floor exercise (Rio 2016)

SILVER (1): Team all-around (Tokyo 2020)

BRONZE (2): Balance beam (Rio 2016), Balance beam (Tokyo 2020)

TOTAL MEDALS:

ABOVE: Simone Biles receives her gold medal on the all-around podium at the 2016 Rio Olympics

GABBY DOUGLAS

Simone Biles, at Rio 2016, was not the first US gymnast to have won both individual all-around and team gold medals at a single Summer's Olympics. That landmark had been achieved by her 2016 team-mate Gabby Douglas – but four years earlier at London 2012. Douglas, who began gymnastic classes as a six-year-old, was 16 when she clinched her two 2012 golds in London's O2 Arena. She was the only member of the US team to compete in all four categories – the vault, uneven bars, balance beam and floor exercise – in the final, as she, McKayla Maroney, captain Aly Raisman, Kyla Ross and Jordyn Wieber took gold. The team, all aged between 15 and 18 that summer, were dubbed the "Fab Five" but chose to call themselves the "Fierce Five" instead – while Douglas' dazzling release skills on the uneven bars has seen her nicknamed "the Flying Squirrel". Douglas and Raisman remained on the team for the Rio 2016 Games where they were joined by Biles, Laurie Hernandez and Madison Kocian and were now being referred to as the "Final Five". Rio 2016 was the last Summer Olympics with artistic gymnastic teams of five, with the number reduced to four from Tokyo 2020 onwards.

ABOVE: Gabby Douglas wins gold in the women's team competition at the 2016 Rio Olympic Games

BORN: December 31, 1995, in Newport News, Virginia

EVENT: Artistic gymnastics

GOLD (3): Team all-around, individual all-around (London 2012), Team (Rio de Janeiro 2016)

TOTAL MEDALS:

GEORGE EYSER

If winning six gold medals at one Olympics was not impressive enough, George Eyser did so with a wooden leg after having been hit by a train as a youngster. All six of his medals at the 1904 Games in St Louis, Missouri, came on October 29 – the same day another American gymnast Anton Heida also won six medals, five golds and a silver. Eyser's triumphs included rope climbing, covering the 7.62m-long rope in 7.0 seconds, ahead of fellow US competitors Charles Krause (7.2) and Emil Voigt (9.8). The only other Olympics to feature rope climbing as a medal event were Athens 1896, Athens 1906, Paris 1924 and Los Angeles 1932. Eyser's wooden leg proved no bar to him also winning gold – shared with Heida – in the vault, which involved judges ranking competitors on their leaps over a long "vaulting horse". He also triumphed in the parallel bars, scoring 44 points for his three exercises – one ahead of Heida. Eyser had been born in Germany but his family moved to the US when he was 14 and he gained American citizenship 10 years later.

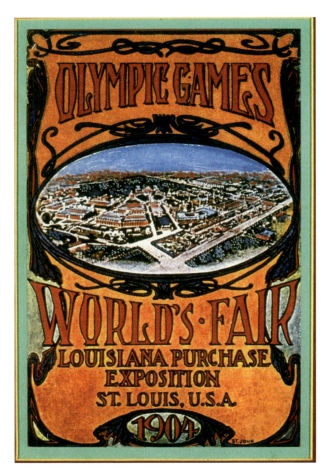

LEFT: George Eyser lines up with the Concordia team in 1908

BORN: August 31, 1870, in Kiel, Germany

DIED: March 6, 1919, aged 48, in Denver Colorado

EVENT: Artistic gymnastics

GOLD (3): Rope climbing, vault, parallel bars (St Louis 1904)

SILVER (2): Combined 4 events, pommel horse (St Louis 1904)

BRONZE (1): Horizontal bar (St Louis 1904)

TOTAL MEDALS:

SHANNON MILLER

LEFT: Poster for the 1904 Summer Olympics in St. Louis, United States

Shannon Miller's success in Barcelona in 1992, her first Olympics, could also be seen as a little bittersweet – she returned to the US with more medals than any of her compatriots that summer while her two silvers and three bronzes also set a record for most medals at a single Games without winning gold. She only missed out on the top prize in the individual all-around final by 0.012 points behind Ukraine's Tatiana Gutsu, the closest-ever Olympics gymnastics winning margin. But Miller put that right four years later in Atlanta, where she helped the US win the team all-around before adding her own individual triumph in the balance beam. Her balance beam score of 9.862 put her ahead of Ukraine's Lilia Podkopayeva in second with 9.825 and Gina Gogean of Romania on 9.787. No US gymnast has more Olympic medals than Miller's seven, although Simone Biles drew level at Tokyo 2020. Miller also has nine Gymnastics World Championships medals and is the only woman inducted in the United States Olympic Hall of Fame twice, for both her team and as an individual.

BORN: March 10, 1977, in Rolla Missouri

EVENT: Artistic gymnastics

GOLD (2): Team all-around, individual balance beam (Atlanta 1996)

SILVER (2): Individual all-around, balance beam (Barcelona 1992)

BRONZE (3): Team all-around, individual uneven bars, floor exercise (Barcelona 1992)

TOTAL MEDALS:

RIGHT: Gymnast and cancer survivor Shannon Miller proudly displays her Olympic medal haul here in 2004

GYMNASTICS 65

CARLY PATTERSON

Carly Patterson went into the individual all-around gymnastics final in Athens in 2004 with five-time world champion Svetlana Khorkina, from Russia, the favourite to win. Patterson had just suffered some disappointment as part of the US team who, having won gold four years earlier in Sydney, had to settle for silver this time in the team all-around – with Patterson suffering wobbles on the balance beam and stubbing her toe while performing on the uneven bars. Khorkina surged into the lead in the individual all-around final with strong displays in the vault and uneven bars rounds, but impressive landings by Patterson in the balance beam and floor events propelled her to top spot with an overall judges' score of 38.387, ahead of Khorkina's 38.211 and China's Nan Zhang on 38.049. Patterson followed this up with silver in the balance beam event, behind Romania's Cătălina Ponor. Patterson was forced to retire just two years later, aged only 18, after bulging discs in her lower back were discovered and went on to pursue an interest in singing. She competed in US television talent show Celebrity Duets later that year and released a debut album, *Back To The Beginning*, three years later.

BORN: February 4, 1988, in Baton Rouge, Louisiana

EVENT: Artistic gymnastics

GOLD (1): Individual all-around (Athens 2004)

SILVER (2): Team all-around, individual balance beam (Athens 2004)

TOTAL MEDALS:

RIGHT: Carly Patterson on the balance beam whilst going for gold in the Individual all-around event, Athens 2004

MARY LOU RETTON

Sixteen-year-old Mary Lou Retton became one of her country's most popular athletes with her performances at the Soviet bloc-boycotted 1984 Summer Olympics in Los Angeles. Her triumph in the women's individual all-around gymnastics made her the first American woman as well as the first from outside Eastern Europe to win that Olympic event. This was despite concerns in the run-up to the Games that she might not be fit enough to compete, following a knee injury which needed an operation to remove torn cartilage just five weeks before the Los Angeles action. In the final she fell behind Ecaterina Szabo from Romania, the only Soviet bloc country taking part in that year's Games. Retton was 0.15 points adrift after the uneven bars and balance beam rounds – only to score perfect 10s in both the floor exercise and vault events to win with an overall score of 79.175, just 0.50 ahead of Szabo's 79.125. Retton won another four medals that summer – two silvers and two bronzes – before retiring two years later. Retton had been inspired as a young girl to take up gymnastics after watching on TV another Romanian, Nadia Comăneci, win three gold medals – and score seven perfect 10.0 scores – at the 1976 Olympics in Montreal.

KERRI STRUG

BORN: November 19, 1977, in Tucson, Arizona

EVENT: Artistic gymnastics

GOLD (1): Team all-around (Atlanta 1996)

BRONZE (1): Team all-around (Barcelona 1992)

TOTAL MEDALS:

The US gymnasts who won the team all-around gold at Atlanta 1996 were given the name the "Magnificent Seven" – but much of the attention after their dramatic triumph was directed towards one of them, Kerri Strug. She had to be carried to the medal podium by coach Béla Károlyi and was wearing a soft cast, after suffering agonising injuries in the moments she was helping her team clinch gold. The US were leading their Russian rivals by 0.897 going into the final rounds, with the Russians on floor exercise and the Americans on vault. Strug was on sixth, after 14-year-old team-mate Dominique Moceanu fell twice and scored poorly. Strug too fell on her first attempt, landing awkwardly on her ankle, before limping to the side and asking Károlyi whether she really needed to carry out her second vault – telling him: "I can't do it. I can't feel my leg." But she was persuaded to have another go, since the Russians could still potentially overtake with their last efforts, and made the jump and landing before crumpling to the floor in pain. Her score of 9.712 was good enough to secure the USA's gold medal and she became a national hero. After receiving her medal she needed hospital treatment for a third-degree lateral sprain and tendon damage – injuries which ruled her out of two individual finals for which she had qualified. She subsequently retired from gymnastics – and went on to run marathons.

ABOVE: Kerri Strug is carried by coach Béla Károlyi, Atlanta 1996

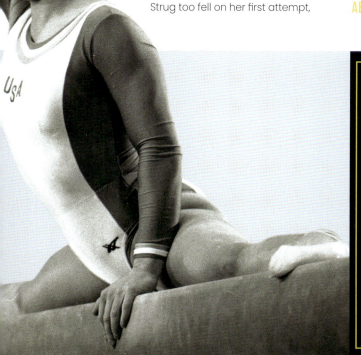

BORN: January 24, 1968, in Fairmont, West Virginia

EVENT: Artistic gymnastics

GOLD (1): All-around (Los Angeles 1984)

SILVER (2): Team all-around, individual vault (Los Angeles 1984)

BRONZE (2): Uneven bars, floor exercise (Los Angeles 1984)

TOTAL MEDALS:

RUGBY

Rugby union was a medal event at four of the first modern Olympics, in 1900, 1908, 1920 and 1924 but the sport disappeared from the Games until returning at Rio 2016. Rugby's return came in a different format – as rugby sevens, with seven players on each side playing seven-minute halves in contrast to rugby union's teams of 15 with 40-minute halves. Pierre de Coubertin, French founder of the modern Olympics, was a rugby fan and refereed the first ever French rugby union championship final in 1892.

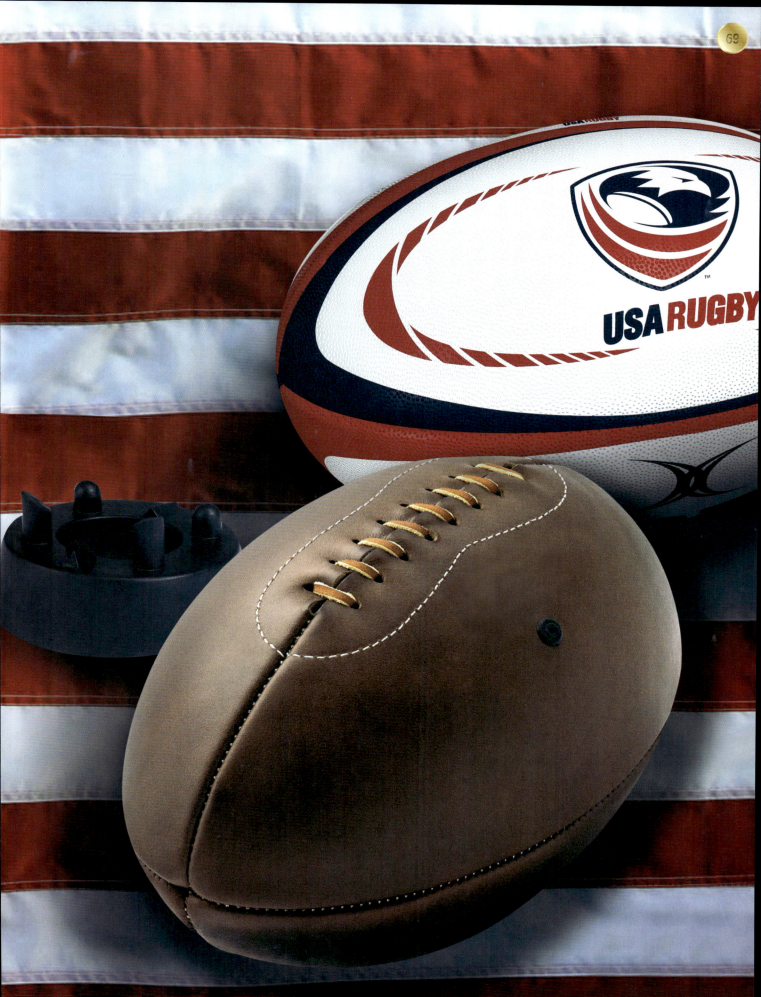

MORRIS KIRKSEY

Rugby union with 15 players on each team has only been an Olympic sport at four Games and none since 1924, though rugby sevens was introduced as an event at Rio 2016. France were the first winners, in Paris in 1900 where Great Britain came second and Germany third, before Australia beat Great Britain 32-3 in the only match at London 1908. The remaining two tournaments saw the US take gold both times, beating France 8-0 in Antwerp in 1920 and topping a three-team table in Paris four years later with France again settling for silver and winless Romania bronze. Leading the American gold medallists in 1920 was Morris Kirksey, who had already that summer won two track and field medals – silver in the 100m, behind compatriot Charley Paddock, and gold as he anchored the US 4 x 100m relay team to victory in a world record time of 42.2 seconds. Alongside Kirksey in the US rugby side was Daniel Carroll, who 12 years earlier had been part of the Australian gold medal-winning team but stayed on in the US after taking part in a rugby tour there in 1912. Carroll is one of only two people to win Olympic gold medals representing two different nations. The other is Georgian-born weightlifter Kakhi Kakhiashvili, for the Unified Team representing Russia in the under-90kg category at Barcelona 1992 and for Greece after becoming a citizen there in the under-99kg and under-94 categories in Atlanta four years later.

ABOVE: Poster of the 1920 Olympic Games. Printed in 17 languages plus French/Dutch bilingual versions

BELOW: One of the 154 (identical) gold medals awarded at the 1920 Antwerp Olympic Games

BORN: September 13, 1895, in Waxahachie, Texas

DIED: November 25, 1981, aged 86, in San Mateo California

EVENTS: Rugby, track and field

GOLD (2): Rugby, 4 x 100m relay (Antwerp 1920)

SILVER (1): 100m (Antwerp 1920)

TOTAL MEDALS:

SHOOTING

Modern Olympics founder Pierre de Coubertin was a former French pistol champion and shooting has played a part at every Games other than 1904 in St Louis and 1928 in Amsterdam. There are now 15 shooting events scheduled for the 2024 Paris Olympics, five apiece in rifle, pistol and shotgun categories – with men's and women's individual tournaments and mixed team events. The number of competitors has been reduced from Tokyo 2020's 360 to 340, 170 men and 170 women.

WILLIS A. LEE

Willis A. Lee and US team-mate Lewis Spooner became the first people to win seven medals at one Olympic Games, when they achieved their hauls – all for shooting – at the 1920 Antwerp Games. All of Lee's medals came in team events – five golds, a silver and a bronze – while Spooner went home with four golds, a silver and two bronzes, one of his third-place finishes coming in the individual military rifle, prone, 600m category. The events challenged shooters to aim at targets a certain number of times from different distances, and within various time periods ranging from a matter of seconds to as long as two hours – scoring points depending on what they hit. Lee had entered the US Naval Academy in 1904, joining the rifle team there, and served during the First World War on the destroyers *USS O'Brien* and *USS Lea*. In 1942 he was promoted to Rear Admiral in the US Navy and was awarded the Naval Cross for his service during that year's Naval Battle of Guadalcanal during the Second World War. His and Spooner's record of seven medals at a single Olympics was only matched 40 years later by USSR gymnast Boris Shakhlin in Rome, before another Soviet gymnast Aleksandr Dityatin claimed eight golds at Moscow 1980.

BORN: May 11, 1888, in Natlee, Kentucky

DIED: August 25, 1945, aged 57, off the coast of Maine

EVENTS: Shooting – small-bore rifle, army rifle, free rifle

GOLD (5): 50m team small-bore rifle, standing; 300m team military rifle, prone; 600m team military rifle, prone; 300 and 600m team military rifle, prone; 300m team free rifle (Antwerp 1920)

SILVER (1): Team 300m army rifle, standing (Antwerp 1920)

BRONZE (1): Team 100m running deer single shots (Antwerp 1920)

TOTAL MEDALS: 🥇🥇🥇🥇🥇🥈🥉

LANNY BASSHAM

SHOOTING

Lanny Bassham's sportsmanship won him admiration as well as a gold medal at the 1976 Olympics in Montreal. By now shooting had become integrated at the Games, with men and women first taking part in the same events in Mexico City in 1968 – only for them to be segregated again from Atlanta 1996 onwards. In Montreal, Bassham tied on 1162 points with fellow American Margaret Murdock in the small bore rifle, three positions event – but he was awarded the gold because he managed three 100s to her two. The event challenged competitors to aim with a .22 rifle at a target 50m away, carrying out 40 shots while prone, 40 kneeling and 40 standing. Despite being declared the winner, Bassham asked for gold medals to be given to both him and Murdock. When this was refused he insisted Murdock join him at the top of the medal podium for the US national anthem. Bassham, a soldier based at Fort Worth in Texas, had previously won silver in the same event at the 1972 Olympics in Munich and took special training on mental discipline under pressure to help him go one better in Montreal. He later wrote books and led courses on his "Mental Management" approach.

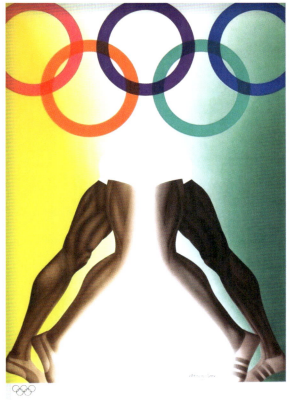

ABOVE: Artwork for one of the 1972 Munich Olympic Games posters

LEFT: Olympic gold medalist Lanny Massham stands with bronze medal winner Werner Seibold after he won the rifle competition at the 1976 Olympics in Montreal

BORN: January 2, 1947, in Comanche, Texas

EVENTS: Shooting – small-bore rifle

GOLD (1): Mixed 50m rifle, three positions (Montreal 1976)

SILVER (1): Mixed 50m rifle, three positions (Munich 1972)

TOTAL MEDALS: 🥇 🥈

MARGARET MURDOCK

Margaret Murdock, who learned to shoot after joining her father at a local firing range as a child, narrowly missed out on qualifying for the US shooting team at the Mexico City Olympics in 1968 – the first Games with mixed shooting events. But she became the first woman to make the team in Montreal eight years later, where she was also the first woman to win a shooting Olympics medal – silver, in the 50m small-bore rifle, three positions event – finishing level on points with Lanny Bassham but losing out on gold due to the tie-break rule counting 100 scores. She had benefitted from that same rule when qualifying for the team in the US trials, having finished level on points with rival John Writer. Nine years before her Olympic breakthrough, Murdock – then competing under her birth name of Margaret Thompson – had been the first woman to set a shooting world record for either sex – scoring 391 for small-bore rifle, kneeling, at the 1967 Pan American Games. After spending four years in the US Army, serving as a shooting instructor and rising to the rank of major, Murdock retired from competitive shooting aged 35 and became a registered nurse specialising in anaesthesia.

RIGHT: Margaret Murdock receives her silver medal at the 1976 Montreal Olympic Games

BORN: August 25, 1942, in Topeka, Kansas

EVENT: Shooting - small-bore rifle

SILVER (1): Montreal 1976

TOTAL MEDALS:

CARL OSBURN

No one has won more Olympics shooting medals than Carl Osburn and, until swimmer Michael Phelps passed him in 2008, no American had more Summer Olympics medals of any kind, though Mark Spitz had equalled his tally in 1972. Osburn, a commander in the US Navy, went to his first Games in Stockholm in 1912 and came back with a team rifle gold – with Great Britain second and hosts Sweden third – as well as his first two individual silvers in the 600m free rifle and the 300m military rifle, three positions. In that 600m free rifle final he finished level on 94 points with France's Paul Colas only to lose 91-90 in a shoot-off for the gold, though another shoot-off did clinch him the silver over Norway's Engebret Skogen in the other event. After the First World War meant no Summer Olympics in 1916, Osburn won another four golds at Paris 1920 including in the individual 300m military rifle, standing category, before adding a final silver in the 600m free rifle in Paris four years later. The year after his death aged 82 in December 1966, Osburn's widow Mary donated his medals, trophies and memorabilia to the Naval Historical Foundation.

LEFT: An official poster of the 1924 Paris Olympic Games

SHOOTING

KIM RHODE

BORN: July 16, 1979, in Whittier, California

EVENTS: Shooting – double trap, skeet

GOLD (3): Double trap (Atlanta 1996), Double trap (Athens 2004), Skeet (London 2012)

SILVER (1): Skeet (Beijing 2008)

BRONZE (2): Double trap (Sydney 2000), Skeet (Rio 2016)

TOTAL MEDALS: 🥇🥇🥇🥈🥉🥉

BORN: November 5, 1884, in Jacksontown, Ohio

DIED: December 28, 1966, aged 82, in St Helena, California

EVENTS: Shooting – military rifle, free rifle

GOLD (5): Team rifle (Stockholm 1912), 300m military rifle, standing; 300m team military rifle, prone; 300 and 600m team military rifle, prone; team free rifle (Antwerp 1920)

SILVER (4): 600m free rifle; 300m military rifle, three positions (Stockholm 1912), 300m team military rifle, standing (Antwerp 1920), 600m free rifle (Paris 1924)

BRONZE (2): 50m team small-bore rifle (Stockholm 1912), 100m team running deer, single shots (Antwerp 1920)

TOTAL MEDALS: 🥇🥇🥇🥇🥇🥈🥈🥈🥈🥉🥉

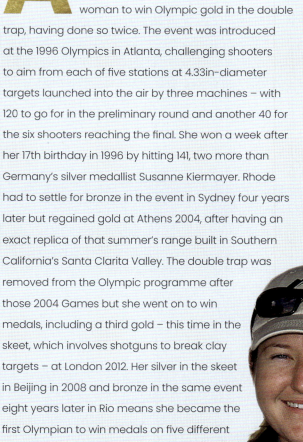

Among the many records achieved by Kim Rhode is one which looks unlikely to be matched – she stands as the first and last woman to win Olympic gold in the double trap, having done so twice. The event was introduced at the 1996 Olympics in Atlanta, challenging shooters to aim from each of five stations at 4.33in-diameter targets launched into the air by three machines – with 120 to go for in the preliminary round and another 40 for the six shooters reaching the final. She won a week after her 17th birthday in 1996 by hitting 141, two more than Germany's silver medallist Susanne Kiermayer. Rhode had to settle for bronze in the event in Sydney four years later but regained gold at Athens 2004, after having an exact replica of that summer's range built in Southern California's Santa Clarita Valley. The double trap was removed from the Olympic programme after those 2004 Games but she went on to win medals, including a third gold – this time in the skeet, which involves shotguns to break clay targets – at London 2012. Her silver in the skeet in Beijing in 2008 and bronze in the same event eight years later in Rio means she became the first Olympian to win medals on five different continents and the first woman to win medals at six successive Olympics.

SOFTBALL

Softball has been played as a women-only event at five Olympic Games – Atlanta 1996, Sydney 2000, Athens 2004, Beijing 2008 and Tokyo 2020, though will not play a part in Paris in 2024. Nor will men's baseball, though both sports could return when Los Angeles hosts the 2028 Summer Olympics. The United States won the first three softball gold medals but were beaten by Japan in both the 2008 and 2020 finals.

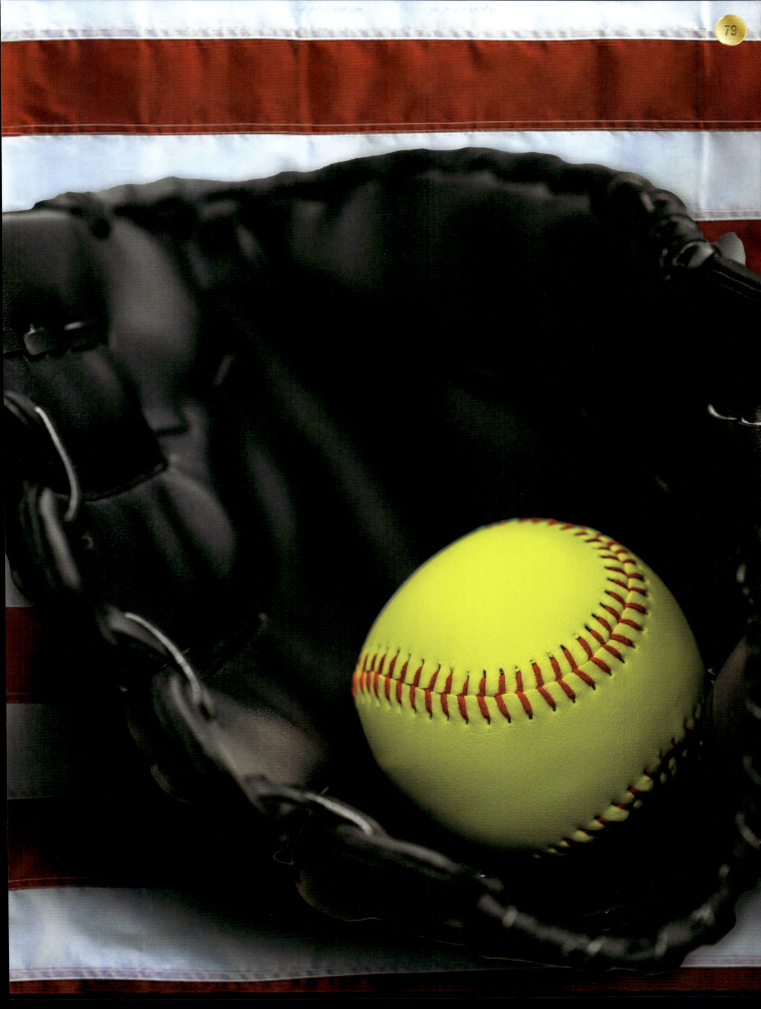

LISA FERNANDEZ

After men's baseball made its Olympics debut in Barcelona in 1992, women's softball was introduced in Atlanta four years later. The USA won the first three gold medals, not only in Atlanta but retaining their titles in Sydney four years later and then in Athens in 2004. A key player each time was inspirational pitcher Lisa Fernandez, making her the only triple Olympic champion in softball. Her father had played baseball in Cuba while her mother and her uncle played a similar game called stickball. Fernandez took up softball as an eight-year-old and went on to lead UCLA in Los Angeles to two national championships in 1990 and 1992 ahead of her international successes. The US won their first five of eight matches at the 1996 Olympics, losing to Australia in their sixth despite Fernandez getting all but one of the opposing batters out, and ultimately beat China 3-1 in the final. Fernandez and the US retained their title in Sydney, this time beating Japan 2-1 to claim gold despite losing their opening three matches of the tournament – and she completed her hat-trick in Athens as the US won all nine games, climaxing in a 5-1 trouncing of Australia. Fernandez played in four of those victories, including the gold medal match.

TOP RIGHT: Athens 2004 Olympic Games official poster

BORN: February 22, 1971, in Long Beach, California

EVENT: Softball

POSITION: Pitcher, third baseman

GOLD (3): Atlanta 1996, Sydney 2000, Athens 2004

TOTAL MEDALS: ●●●

SOFTBALL

JENNIE FINCH

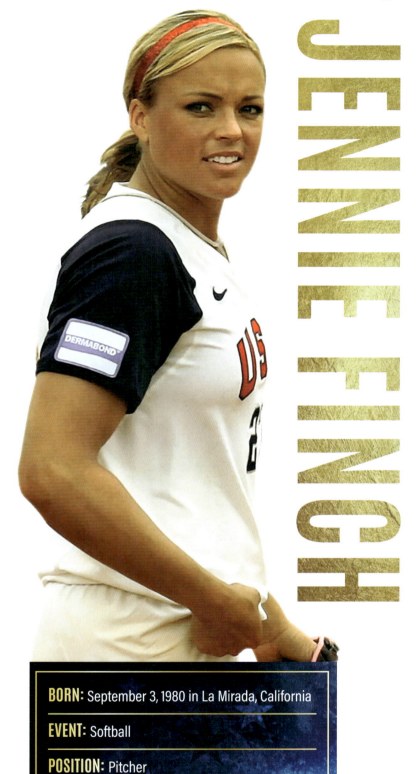

Australia's solitary run in their 5-1 defeat to the US in the 2004 softball final at the 2004 Athens Olympics was the first and only one conceded by the gold medallists in their nine matches that summer. Pitching duties were shared in Athens between Lisa Fernandez and Jennie Finch, who has been described by *Time* magazine as the most famous softball player in history. The devoutly-Christian Finch was also a member of the USA's silver medal-winning squad in Sydney four years later where she apologised for them letting the nation down following a surprise 3-1 defeat to Japan in the final – the American players' first loss in 22 matches. The 2008 Olympics looked like being the last time softball featured, after the International Olympic Committee announced in 2005 it was being dropped from the Games – but it did return at Tokyo 2020, where Japan again beat the US in the final, this time 2-0. Finch retired in 2010 with a record of 38 US victories credited to her as a pitcher, against just two defeats. She was among the campaigners for softball to be restored to the Olympics. Men's baseball was also brought back for Tokyo 2020, with Japan also winning gold here after beating the US 2-0 in the final but – like softball – it will not be played at Paris 2024, though both could return for the 2028 Games in Los Angeles.

BELOW: One of the posters used at the 2008 Beijing Olympics

BORN: September 3, 1980 in La Mirada, California

EVENT: Softball

POSITION: Pitcher

GOLD (1): Athens 2004

SILVER (1): Beijing 2008

TOTAL MEDALS: 🥇🥈

SURFING

Surfing made its Olympics debut at Tokyo 2020, with an event apiece for men and women. Surfers ride waves on their boards and are scored by judges on how well they perform and the difficulty of their manoeuvres. Surfing at the 2024 Paris Olympics will take place not in France, but at the Teahupo'o reef pass in Tahiti, French Polynesia – 9,800 miles away from Paris, making it the farthest place from a host city for an Olympics medal contest to take place.

OLYMPIC LEGENDS USA

CARISSA MOORE

Surfing made its Olympics debut at Tokyo 2020 and is scheduled to continue in Paris. The first gold medal winner in the women's shortboard event was 28-year-old Hawaiian Carissa Moore, who took the gold for the US with a final score of 14.93 against South Africa's Bianca Buitendag on 8.46. Competitors were judged on how they handled their two best waves, based on factors such as difficulty, power, speed and variety. That same year, 2021, Moore won her fifth World Surf League women's title for the fifth time – her first being ten years earlier when aged just 18, the youngest surfer to become world champion. She competes in world events under the Hawaiian flag, as those competitions permit, but was under the US banner when winning Olympic gold. Two-time world champion John "John John" Florence was among the favourites in the men's softboard event at Tokyo 2020 but was knocked out in the third round by US team-mate Kolohe Andino who was himself eliminated in the next round, the quarter-finals, by Japan's eventual silver medallist Kanoa Igarashi as Brazil's Ítalo Ferreira took gold.

BORN: August 27, 1992, in Honolulu, Hawaii

EVENT: Surfing - shortboard

GOLD (1): Tokyo 2020

TOTAL MEDALS:

SURFING 85

ABOVE: Carissa Moore, center, holding her gold medal, South Africa's Bianca Buitendag, left and Japan's Amuro Tsuzuki bronze medal celebrate on the podium

MAIN IMAGE: Carissa Moore during the quarterfinals of the women's surfing competition at the 2020 Summer Olympics, Tuesday, July 27, 2021

TENNIS

After being played at every Summer Olympics between 1896 and 1924, tennis was dropped as a medal event until 1988 in Seoul – though it did feature as a demonstration sport in Mexico City in 1968 and Los Angeles 16 years later. The playing surface used varies between Olympics – predominantly hard courts have been used, though London 2012 was on grass and the Paris events are on clay as they were in Barcelona in 1992.

ANDRE AGASSI

OLYMPIC LEGENDS USA

BORN: April 29, 1970, in Las Vegas, Nevada
EVENT: Tennis – men's singles
GOLD (1): Atlanta 1996
TOTAL MEDALS:

The first two tennis men's singles winners after the sport returned as an Olympics medal event in 1988 in Seoul were Miloslav Mečíř, of what was then Czechoslovakia, and in 1992 Switzerland's Marc Rosset at Barcelona. Neither would ever win a Grand Slam singles title in their careers. However, the 1996 Olympic champion was a far more familiar figure in Andre Agassi. He had won his first Grand Slam at Wimbledon in 1992, despite having previously complained about the traditional event as too stuffy for him at a time when he was iconic for his colourful clothing, long hair and earring. He would end his career with eight Grand Slam titles, on three different surfaces, and was the first man to have won all five of Wimbledon, the Australian Open, the French Open, the US Open and the Olympics – the career "Golden Slam". His 1996 triumph in Atlanta culminated in a comfortable victory over Spain's Sergi Bruguera in the final, Agassi needing just 77 minutes to win 6-2, 6-3, 6-1. Agassi's father Emmanuel "Mike" Agassi had represented Iran as a boxer at the 1948 Olympics in London and the Games in Helsinki four years later, losing in the first round each time. In 2001 Agassi married fellow tennis star Steffi Graf, who had won Olympics gold for West Germany in the women's singles in 1988 as well as bronze in the women's doubles before silver in the singles in Barcelona four years later.

JENNIFER CAPRIATI

Until returning at Seoul in 1988, the last appearance of tennis at the Summer Olympics had been in Paris in 1924, where the US enjoyed a clean sweep of golds. Vincent Richards won the men's singles and the men's doubles with Frank Hunter, while the women's singles title went to Helen Wills who teamed up with Hazel Wightman to triumph in the women's doubles. Mixed doubles gold went to Wightman and Richard "Dick" Norris Williams, who 12 years earlier had survived the sinking of the *Titanic* which killed his father Charles Duane Williams. In 1992 in Barcelona 16-year-old American Jennifer Capriati became the country's first female Olympic champion since Wills. She shocked reigning champion Steffi Graf of Germany in the final despite losing the first set, coming back to triumph 3-6, 6-3, 6-4. Capriati, who turned professional aged 13, had beaten the No.2 seed Arantxa Sánchez-Vicario of Spain in the semi-finals. The New Yorker took time off from tennis in 1994, struggling with personal issues, but later returned and went on to win three Grand Slams – the Australian Open and French Open in 2001 and the Australian Open again the following year.

BELOW: Jennifer Capriati celebrates receiving the gold medal at the 1992 Barcelona Summer Olympics

BORN: March 29, 1976, in New York City, New York
EVENT: Tennis – women's singles
GOLD (1): Barcelona 1992
TOTAL MEDALS:

SERENA WILLIAMS

OLYMPIC LEGENDS USA

Serena Williams has been one of the most dominant players in tennis history. Only Australia's Margaret Court, with 24 in the 1960s and 1970s, won more than her 23 Grand Slam single's titles – not to mention Williams's 14 doubles Grand Slams alongside elder sister Venus. The siblings have also won Olympics gold three times together, at Sydney 2000, Beijing 2008 and London 2012 – the only blip being a first-round defeat to China's eventual gold medallists Li Ting and Sun Tiantian in Athens in 2004. Serena was hampered by a left knee injury that summer. They just dropped one set in the Sydney 2000 tournament before beating Dutch pair Kristie Boogert and Miriam Oremans, before later finals brought similarly-one-sided victories – 6-2, 6-0 against Spain's Anabel Medina Garrigues and Virginia Ruano Pascual in 2008 and 6-4, 6-4 versus the Czech Republic's Andrea Sestini Hlaváčková and Lucie Hradecká four years later. London 2012 saw the Williams sisters become the first tennis players to win four Olympic gold medals – Venus had won the singles title at Sydney 2000 and now Serena won her first, dismissing long-time rival Russia's Maria Sharapova 6-0, 6-1 in the London final at Wimbledon. A month earlier Serena had won the Wimbledon women's singles title at the same venue and the sisters the women's double crown. Serena has won the Wimbledon singles tournament seven times, Venus on five occasions, with six doubles triumphs for the pair.

ABOVE: Serena Williams playing against Daria Gavrilova of Australia in their first-round match on Day 2 of the Rio 2016 Olympic Games

BORN: September 26, 1981, in Saginaw, Michigan

EVENTS: Tennis – women's singles, women's doubles

GOLD (4): Women's doubles (Sydney 2000), Women's doubles (Beijing 2008), Women's singles, women's doubles (London 2012)

TOTAL MEDALS: 🥇🥇🥇🥇

VENUS WILLIAMS

Venus and Serena Williams were trained to be future tennis superstars from a young age by parents Richard Williams and Oracene Price. Venus, 15 months the elder, was the first of them to win Wimbledon – beating fellow American Lindsay Davenport in the 2000 final in July that year – and followed that up with a first Olympic singles gold in Sydney the following month, defeating Russia's Elena Dementieva 6-2, 6-4 in the final. As well as the three women's doubles golds she would claim with sister Serena that summer as well as at Beijing 2008 and London 2012, she added a fifth medal of her own in Rio in 2016. This time it was silver as she teamed up with Rajeev Ram but lost an all-American final to Bethanie Mattek-Sands and Jack Sock. The deciding third set was a "super tie-break" to ten points, which Mattek-Sands and Sock took 10-7. Venus and Serena had been knocked out in the first round of the Rio 2016 women's doubles while Serena reached just the third round of the singles. Venus's ten Grand Slam single's titles include five at Wimbledon, while the sisters have faced each other nine times in Grand Slam finals – with Serena winning seven.

BORN: June 17, 1980, in Lynwood, California

EVENTS: Tennis – women's singles, women's doubles, mixed doubles

GOLD (4): Women's singles, Women's doubles (Sydney 2000), Women's doubles (Beijing 2008), Women's doubles (London 2012)

SILVER (1): Mixed doubles (Rio 2016)

TOTAL MEDALS: 🥇🥇🥇🥇🥈

TRACK AND FIELD

Athletics tends to provide the most watched and keenly anticipated events at any Summer Olympics and offers the most medals – with 48 events across track and field, road running and race walking scheduled for the 2024 Games in Paris. Most are held within the host nation's dedicated Olympic stadium, featuring a 400m-length running track and a field in the middle for events such as the high jump, long jump and triple jump and throwing sports discus and javelin.

EVELYN ASHFORD

Evelyn Ashford overcame boycott disappointment and repeated injury setbacks to become a four-time Olympic champion – and the fastest woman in the world along the way. Ashford finished fifth as a 19-year-old in the 100m final at Montreal 1976 but had high hopes of winning gold in Moscow four years later – only for the US to boycott the event. She set a world record time of 10.79 seconds in June 1983 but pulled a hamstring and fell in the 100m final of that year's inaugural World Championships in Helsinki, Finland. The following summer Ashford finally won gold at the 1984 Los Angeles Games with an Olympic record 10.97. Worries about her right hamstring forced her to pull out of the 200m but she claimed a second gold as the finisher for the US team in the 4 x 100m. Later that year she set a new world best for the 100m, running it in 10.76. Ashford again completed a 4 x 100m win for the US in Seoul four years later, despite a messy baton handover with Florence Griffith Joyner who had beaten her to gold that summer in the 100m final – and Ashford completed a hat-trick of 4 x 100m triumphs in Barcelona in 1992. She is one of only six women to win four track and field Olympic golds.

BORN: April 15, 1957, in Shreveport, Louisiana

EVENT: 100m

GOLD (4): 100m, 4 x 100m relay (Los Angeles 1984) 4 x 100m relay (Seoul 1988) 4 x 100m relay (Barcelona 1992)

SILVER (1): 100m (Seoul 1988)

TOTAL MEDALS: 🥇🥇🥇🥇🥈

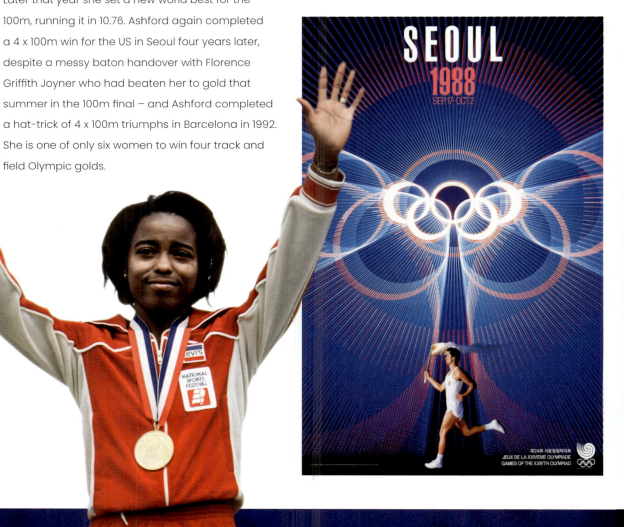

BELOW: One of the official posters of the 1988 Seoul Summer Olympics

BOB BEAMON

TRACK AND FIELD

Bob Beamon stunned the world with his immense performance in the long jump at the 1968 Summer Olympics in Mexico City. His huge leap of 8.9m set a world record – beating the existing best by a full 55cm – and stood for another 23 years until finally broken by fellow American Mike Powell. Yet it remains an Olympic record. He had come close to missing out on the final, overstepping in his first two attempts during qualifying – only to reconsider his approach run. US team-mate Ralph Boston advised him to take off several inches before the board, which he did cleanly to clinch his place in the next stage where he went on to make history – and also inspire the adjective "Beamonesque", for doing something which raises the bar by a vast margin. The previous world record had been held by Boston, jointly with Russia's Igor Ter-Ovanesyan. It took some time after Beamon's momentous leap before he realised just what he had achieved – though Great Britain's defending Olympic champion Lynn Davies, looking on, told him: "You have destroyed this event." A new optical measuring device being used ran out of rail so officials had to use an old-fashioned steel tape to record just how far Beamon's jump had taken him. Beamon followed up the Mexico City Games by attempting a shift into basketball, before going into motivational speaking, social work and coaching.

BELOW: Bob Beamon setting the Olympic record at the 1968 Games in Mexico City

BORN: August 29, 1946, in South Jamaica, Queens, New York

EVENT: Long jump

GOLD (1): Mexico City 1968

TOTAL MEDALS: 🥇

JOAN BENOIT

The men's marathon has been run at every Olympics since the first modern Games in Athens in 1896 but the women's race was only introduced in 1984 in Los Angeles, where the USA's Joan Benoit became the first gold medallist. She completed the course in a winning two hours, 24 minutes and 22 seconds, despite having gone into the Games with injury concerns. She needed arthroscopic right knee surgery in March that year just 17 days before the US qualification trials yet managed to win through. In the Olympics marathon she took the lead and pulled away from the field after just 14 minutes and finished 400m and 84 seconds ahead of Norway's Grete Waitz. The previous year Benoit had broken Waitz's existing world record by running the Boston Marathon in 2:22:43 – and a wall mural portraying the moment she crossed the finishing line in Boston was among the sights she passed while surging through the Los Angeles streets on her way to Olympic glory. She went on to win the Chicago Marathon in 1985 though injuries hampered any hopes of returning to the Olympics. In 2019 she marked the 40th anniversary of her first Boston Marathon by running it again, this time alongside daughter Abby – and was satisfied with her time of 3:04:00 at the age of 61.

BORN: May 16, 1957, in Cape Elizabeth, Maine
EVENT: Marathon
GOLD (1): Los Angeles 1984
TOTAL MEDALS: 🥇

LEFT: Joan Benoit comes into the Coliseum to run the last portion of the Women's marathon on the track at the Olympic Games in Los Angeles. She won the gold medal

TRACK AND FIELD

VALERIE BRISCO-HOOKS

Valerie Brisco-Hooks was motivated by the tragic loss of her brother to achieve Olympic immortality. Aspiring athlete Robert was hit and killed by a stray bullet while training on a Los Angeles running track. His sister was just 14 at the time and later said she vowed then to succeed in athletics herself to honour his memory, declaring: "Someone has to carry on the family name, so they chose me." She struggled with weight gain after giving birth to a daughter in 1982 but recovered well enough for the 1984 Olympics in Los Angeles where she had grown up, to win gold in both the 200m and 400m – the first person ever to manage that double at a single Games. She completed a hat-trick of golds as part of the US 4 x 400m team, before adding silver in the same event in Seoul four years later. The Los Angeles Memorial Coliseum stadium where Brisco-Hooks won her three golds in 1994 was just three miles away from where her brother had died 10 years earlier. She set Olympic records in both the 200m and 400m finals that year, respectively 21.81 and 48.83 – times which were precisely equalled in Barcelona eight years later, by the USA's Gwendolyn Torrence in the 200m and France's Marie-José Pérec in the 400m.

BORN: July 6, 1960, in Greenwood, Mississippi

EVENTS: 200m, 400m

GOLD (3): 200m, 400m, 4 x 400m (Los Angeles 1984)

SILVER (1): 4 x 400m (Seoul 1988)

TOTAL MEDALS: 🥇🥇🥇🥈

THOMAS BURKE

Thomas Burke was not only the first person to win the Olympics 100m but repeated the feat in the 400m, at the inaugural modern Games in Athens in 1896 – starting his races from what was at the time an unusual crouching position and which needed special permission from officials in Athens. Burke had qualified alongside another runner from Boston, Thomas Curtis, who opted out of the final to preserve himself for the 110m hurdles in which he too won gold. There were also medals for fellow Americans in Burke's two finals – bronze for Francis Lane in the 100m, silver for Herbert Jamison in the 400m. Lane had finished first in the opening heat of the 100m event, making him the first person to win a race at a modern Olympics as well as the first American to compete. The following year Burke helped set up and was the official starter for the first Boston Marathon, inspired by the event he had witnessed in Athens, and later worked as an athletics coach as well as being a lawyer and journalist.

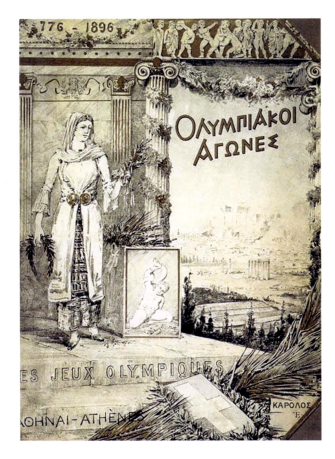

ABOVE: Cover of the official report of the 1896 Athens Summer Olympics

BORN: January 15, 1875, in Boston, Massachusetts

DIED: February 14, 1929, aged 54, in Boston, Massachusetts

EVENTS: 100m, 400m

GOLD (2): 100m, 400m (Athens 1896)

TOTAL MEDALS: 🥇🥇

JAMES CONNOLLY

The honour of being the first Olympic champion, since the modern Games began in 1896, rests with US triple jumper James Connolly, whose leap of 13.71 gave him victory in the final event of that Athens Games' opening day. Simply getting there had been an ordeal for Connolly, whose application for a leave of absence from his studies at Harvard University was denied, prompting him to drop out and travel anyway. After making it to Europe on a freighter he was robbed during a stopover in the Italian city of Naples but managed to chase after the thief and retrieve his ticket to Athens. Once safely there he followed up his triple jump success with second place in the high jump and third place in the long jump, with those two events won by fellow American and Harvard student Ellery Clark, who remains the only person to win both high jump and long jump at the Olympics. Connolly returned to Europe for the 1900 Games in Paris where he came second in the triple jump, before becoming a writer and covering the 1904 Olympics in St Louis and those in London four years later as a journalist – producing one piece entitled: "The English as Poor Loser".

BELOW: James Connolly at the 1896 Olympics

BORN: October 28, 1868, in Boston, Massachusetts

DIED: January 20, 1957, aged 88, in Brookline, Massachusetts

EVENTS: High jump, long jump, triple jump

GOLD (1): Triple jump (Athens 1896)

SILVER (2): High jump (Athens 1896), Triple jump (Paris 1900)

BRONZE (1): Long jump (Athens 1896)

TOTAL MEDALS: 🥇🥈🥈🥉

RAY EWRY

There were fears as a child that Ray Ewry might never walk again – let along go on to leap his way to Olympic greatness. The boy born in Lafayette, Indiana, was diagnosed with polio at the age of five and appeared paralysed, confined to a wheelchair. Yet a rigorous regime of exercise managed to gradually strengthen his leg muscles and he not only managed to stand and walk again but developed into a strapping, successful athlete first at Purdue University in Indiana and then as a member of the New York Athletics Club. He would win eight Olympic gold medals – in the standing high jump, standing long jump and standing triple jump in Paris in 1900 and in St Louis four years later, before again retaining his standing high jump and standing long jump titles at London 1908. The standing triple jump event was abandoned after 1904 and the other two after 1912. No one has won more Olympic medals with a 100 per cent record than Ewry's eight golds. In Paris, where the then-26-year-old was dubbed "The Human Frog", Ewry cleared a world record 1.655m in the high jump – which would have been good enough for second place in the running high jump event in Athens four years earlier.

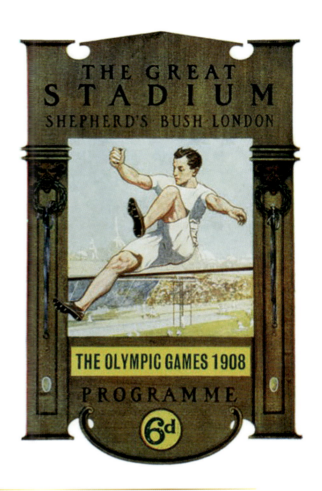

ABOVE: Programme from the 1908 London Olympic Games

BELOW LEFT: Ray Ewry in practice at the 1908 London Olympics

BORN October 14, 1873, in Lafayette, Indiana

DIED: September 29, 1937, aged 63, in Long Island, New York

EVENTS: Standing high jump, standing long jump, standing triple jump

GOLD (8): Standing high jump, standing long jump, standing triple jump (Paris 1900), Standing high jump, standing long jump, standing triple jump (St Louis 1904), Standing high jump, standing long jump (London 1908)

TOTAL MEDALS: 🥇🥇🥇🥇🥇🥇🥇🥇

GAIL DEVERS

Both the women's 100m finals in Barcelona in 1992 and in Atlanta four years later were so closely run that photo-finishes were needed to identify the winner – and both times that proved to be Gail Devers. She finished in 10.82 seconds in Barcelona, ahead of Jamaica's Juliet Cuthbert in 10.83 – then in Atlanta both Devers and another Jamaican, Merlene Ottey, were both timed as crossing the finishing line at 10.94 ahead of the USA's Gwendolyn Torrence in third with 10.96. Devers was judged to have won by 2cm, in an echo of the 1993 World Championships in which she was also declared the winner when she and Ottey both ran the 100m final in 10.82 seconds. Devers' favoured race was actually the 100m hurdles but she missed out on medals in that event at all five of her Olympics, which also took in Seoul 1988, Sydney 2000 and Athens 2004. Her gold medal triumphs – also including 4 x 100m relay triumph in Atlanta – came despite being diagnosed with autoimmune sickness Graves' disease in 1990, which required radiation treatment which left Devers briefly unable to walk – only to recover in time for Barcelona glory, with more to follow.

BORN: November 19, 1966, in Seattle, Washington

EVENTS: 100m, 100m hurdles

GOLD (3): 100m (Barcelona 1992), 100m, 4 x 100m (Atlanta 1996)

TOTAL MEDALS: 🥇🥇🥇

ALLYSON FELIX

No American track and field athlete has won more Olympic medals than sprinter Allyson Felix's 11 – and no track and field athlete in the world has clinched more Olympic golds than her seven, from across five different Games. Felix – nicknamed "Chicken Legs" at school for her skinniness – began with 200m silver in Athens in 2004 aged 18, followed by the same again four years later in Beijing – both times beaten by Jamaica's Veronica Campbell. Felix finally won that race in London 2012, pulling away in the last 50m to finish in 21.88 seconds – her long-time rival, now known as Veronica Campbell Brown, this time coming in fourth. By this point Felix had also taken up the 400m and won relay gold not only in London but also at the two subsequent Olympics in Rio four years later and Tokyo 2020. That Rio 2016 triumph came only after the US team was disqualified in the semi-finals after Felix dropped the baton when handing over to English Gardner, but they were reprieved after footage showed she had been accidentally impeded by another runner. Felix also has an all-time record of 20 World Athletics Championships medals, including 14 golds.

BELOW: The poster design from the 2016 Rio Olympic Games

BORN: November 18, 1985, in Los Angeles, California

EVENTS: 100m, 200m, 400m

GOLD (7): 4 x 400m relay (Beijing 2008), 200m, 4 x 100m, 4 x 400m (London 2012), 4 x 100m, 4 x 400m (Rio 2016), 4 x 400m (Tokyo 2020)

SILVER (3): 200m (Athens 2004), 200m (Beijing 2008), 400m (Rio 2016)

BRONZE (1): 400m (Tokyo 2020)

TOTAL MEDALS:

TRACK AND FIELD

DICK FOSBURY

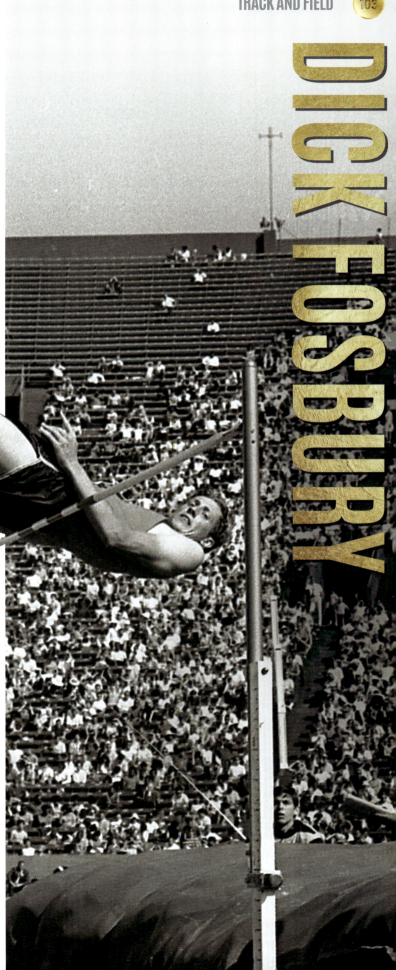

Dick Fosbury did not just win Olympic high jump gold in Mexico City in 1968 – he revolutionised the event and changed the way anyone would approach it in future. Traditionally high jumpers would dive face-down over the pole, in what was known as the "straddle" method. But Fosbury chose instead to swivel at the last moment of his diagonal run-up and hurdle over the bar "back-first" on to the mat – a manoeuvre which gained the nickname, the "Fosbury flop". Fosbury had been experimenting with his approach as a schoolboy athlete because he struggled to master the "straddle" technique – eventually convincing his sceptical coaches his approach was best, while continuing to refine it. In Mexico City he clinched gold by clearing 2.24m at the third attempt, something beyond US team-mate Ed Caruthers who had to settle for silver. Fosbury suffered a series of injuries and did not return to the Olympics, but did win the US national collegiate title in 1969. His lasting influence remains, with Fosbury's technique since adopted by the vast majority of Olympics high jump medallists. He died aged 76 in March 2023 after a recurrence of lymphoma which he first had diagnosed and treated 15 years earlier.

RIGHT: Fosbury at the 1968 U.S. Olympic trials

BORN: March 6, 1947, in Portland, Oregon

DIED: March 12, 2023, aged 76, in Salt Lake City, Utah

EVENT: High jump

GOLD (1): Mexico City 1968

TOTAL MEDALS:

OLYMPIC LEGENDS USA

JUSTIN GATLIN

Controversy has long dogged Justin Gatlin, following not one but two bans for failing drugs tests, but he has a haul of Olympics medals and is in the record books as the fifth fastest sprinter of all time with a 100m personal best of 9.74 seconds. Gatlin was just 19 when he tested positive for amphetamines at the 2001 US Junior World Championships and banned for two years, though this was later halved by the International Amateur Athletic Federation – now World Athletics – after it was ruled they came from medication he was taking for attention deficit disorder. After returning to international competition he was a surprise winner of Olympic 100m gold at the 2004 Games in Athens, finishing in 9.85 – just one-hundredth of a second ahead of Portugal's Francis Obikwelu. In May 2006 Gatlin ran what was initially said to be a new world record in the 100m of 9.76 though his time of 9.766 was instead rounded up to 9.77 – level with the existing best set by Jamaica's Asafa Powell. Gatlin was suspended again that year after testing positive for testosterone. He insisted he was innocent but accepted an eight-year ban, later reduced to four, before going on to win Olympic medals but finishing behind Jamaica's all-conquering Usain Bolt at both London 2012 and Rio 2016.

RIGHT: Justin Gatlin attends the Men's 200m Round 1 during the athletics competition at the Rio 2016 Olympic Games at the Olympic Stadium in Rio de Janeiro

BORN: February 10, 1982, in Brooklyn, New York

EVENTS: 100m, 200m

GOLD (1): 100m (Athens 2004)

SILVER (2): 4 x 100m (Athens 2004), 100m (Rio 2016)

BRONZE (2): 200m (Athens 2004), 100m (London 2012)

TOTAL MEDALS: 🥇🥈🥈🥉🥉

MAURICE GREENE

After showing early promise as a sprinter at school, Maurice Greene only made the 100m quarter-finals at his first World Athletics Championships in 1995, and then missed out on making the US team for the following year's Olympics in Atlanta. Watching tearfully from the crowd in the Centennial Olympic Stadium, he vowed to his father to be taking part next time and soon linked up with the new HSI elite track and field training team. He served notice ahead of the 2000 Sydney Olympics by setting a 100m world record of 9.79 in June 1999 and went on to win Olympic gold in Australia in both the 100m and the 4 x 100m where he finished the race after legs run by US team-mates Jon Drummond, Bernard Williams and Brian Lewis. Greene suffered with injuries in the coming years, including a broken leg from a motorbike accident in 2002, but won further relay medals at Athens 2004 and in Beijing four years later just before retiring. The US had been favourites to retain their 4 x 100m title in Athens but despite a strong finish by Greene they finished in 38.08 seconds, behind Great Britain's 38.07 – the Olympics' closest relay finish.

BORN: July 23, 1974, in Kansas City, Kansas

EVENTS: 100m, 200m

GOLD (2): 100m, 4 x 100m (Sydney 2000)

SILVER (1): 4 x 100m (Athens 2004)

BRONZE (1): 100m (Athens 2004)

TOTAL MEDALS: 🥇🥇🥈🥉

OLYMPIC LEGENDS USA

FLORENCE GRIFFITH JOYNER

BORN: December 21, 1959, in Los Angeles, CA
DIED: Sept 21, 1998, aged 38, in Mission Viejo, CA
EVENT: 100m, 200m
GOLD (3): 100m, 200, 4 x 100m (Seoul 1988)
SILVER (2): 200m (LA 1984), 4 x 400m (Seoul 1988)
TOTAL MEDALS:

Florence Griffith Joyner became a sensation at the 1988 Olympics in Seoul, attracting attention for her colourful running suits, her long painted fingernails – and of course her blistering times as she sprinted to three golds, setting new Olympic and world records as she went. Competing as Florence Griffith, she had won 200m silver at the 1984 Games in Los Angeles but devoted herself to a new training regime ahead of the Seoul Olympics – and set a 100m world record of 10.49 at the US qualifying trials. Griffith Joyner, a former bank teller, ran the 1988 100m final in 10.54 seconds, ahead of US team-mate Evelyn Ashford. Meanwhile, in the 200m the semi-final run by the athlete dubbed "Flo-Jo" was a world record 21.56 before she bested that in the final – clinching gold in just 21.34 seconds. She added another gold in the 4 x 100m but abruptly retired the following February aged just 30. She died in her sleep in September 1998 at the age of 38, having suffered an epileptic seizure. Her widower Al Joyner, who she married in 1987, had previously won triple jump gold for the US at the 1984 Olympics and was her coach ahead of the Seoul Games. Griffith Joyner's 100m and 200m world records both still stand.

BRUCE JENNER

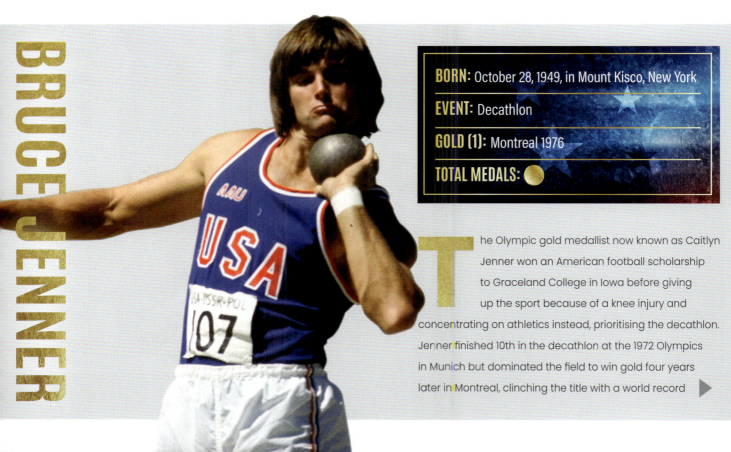

BORN: October 28, 1949, in Mount Kisco, New York
EVENT: Decathlon
GOLD (1): Montreal 1976
TOTAL MEDALS:

The Olympic gold medallist now known as Caitlyn Jenner won an American football scholarship to Graceland College in Iowa before giving up the sport because of a knee injury and concentrating on athletics instead, prioritising the decathlon. Jenner finished 10th in the decathlon at the 1972 Olympics in Munich but dominated the field to win gold four years later in Montreal, clinching the title with a world record

MICHAEL JOHNSON

BORN: September 13, 1967, in Dallas, Texas

EVENTS: 200m, 400m

GOLD (4): 4 x 400m relay (Barcelona 1992), 200m, 400m (Atlanta 1996), 400m (Sydney 2000)

TOTAL MEDALS: ● ● ● ● ○

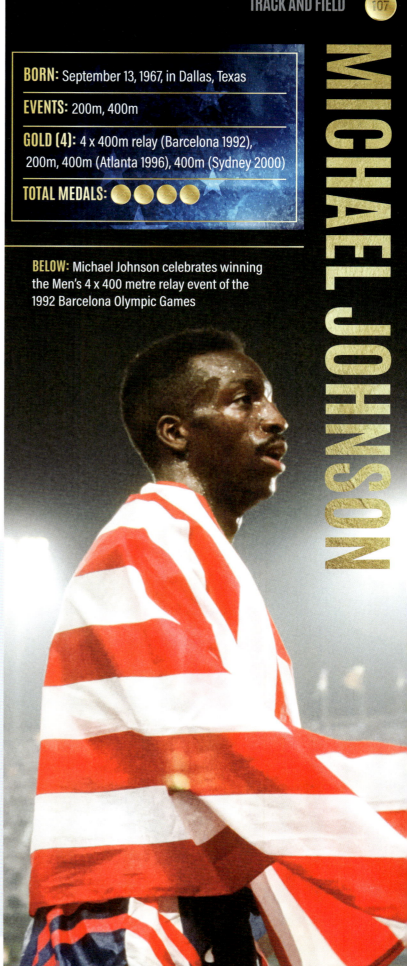

BELOW: Michael Johnson celebrates winning the Men's 4 x 400 metre relay event of the 1992 Barcelona Olympic Games

Michael Johnson just missed out on becoming the first person to win both 200m and 400m gold at a single Olympics – but only by about 15 minutes. France's Marie-José Pérec achieved the feat by adding women's 200m triumph to her 400m success just before Johnson lined up for his 200m final at the 1996 Games in Atlanta, having already won his 400m final in a new Olympics record of 43.49 seconds. This time he recovered from an opening stumble out of the blocks to power through – in his unusual stiff-backed upright running style – in a 200m world record time of 19.32, knocking .34 seconds of the previous best Johnson himself had set. Johnson carried out his victory lap with an ice bag wrapped around his right hamstring – while on his feet were special golden trainers made for him by Nike. Johnson had been hampered at the Barcelona Olympics four years earlier by food poisoning, going out in the 200m semi-finals, though he did help the US to gold in the 4 x 400m relay. He suffered a thigh injury during his 200m race in the US qualifying trials for the 2000 Olympics in Sydney but managed to retain his 400m title, though another 4 x 400m gold was later rescinded because of team-mates' doping offences.

score of 8,618 points. Jenner set personal bests in eight of the ten events: 100m, long jump, shot put, high jump, 400m, pole vault, javelin and 1500m, the other two being 100m hurdles and discus. Defending champion Mykola Avilov of the USSR, whose performance in 1972 had inspired Jenner to take up a much tougher new training regime, took bronze behind Germany's silver medallist Guido Kratschmer. Jenner celebrated by waving an American flag during his lap of honour, after being given it by a spectator – a custom now commonplace among Olympic champions. Jenner, dubbed an "all-American hero", had no intention of continuing as an athlete and became a familiar TV personality – including appearances on 21st-century reality show At Home With The Kardashians after marrying Kris Kardashian in 1991, later divorcing in 2014. The following year Jenner publicly came out as a transgender woman, completed sex reassignment therapy in 2017 and is now known as Caitlyn Jenner.

OLYMPIC LEGENDS USA

JACKIE JOYNER-KERSEE

Few sporting all-rounders can compare with the feats achieved by Jackie Joyner-Kersee – named after former US first lady Jacqueline Kennedy. She only just missed out on heptathlon gold at the 1984 Olympics in Los Angeles, falling short by just 0.06 in the final 800m event, but went one better not only in Seoul four years later but again in Barcelona in 1992 – making her the first heptathlete to win Olympic gold twice in a row. In Seoul she also won the USA's first ever gold in the women's long jump, leaping an Olympic record 7.40m, while her 7,291 points in that summer's heptathlon remains a world record. That heptathlon triumph involved running the 100m hurdles in 12.69 seconds, the 200m in 22.56 and the 800m in 2:08.51, covering 1.86m in the high jump and 7.27m in the long jump, and throwing 15.80m in the shot put and 45.66m in the javelin. Despite suffering from a right hamstring injury she added bronze in the long jump at the 1996 Olympics in Atlanta before enjoying a brief professional basketball career later that year, playing for the Richmond Rage. Her brother was 1984 Olympic triple jump gold medallist Al Joyner and her husband Bob Kersee was also her coach, though said she could only use his surname when she broke a world record – which she first did in July 1986 when breaking the 7,000-point mark in the heptathlon event at the Goodwill Games in Moscow.

BORN: March 3, 1962, in East St Louis, Illinois
EVENTS: Heptathlon, long jump
GOLD (3): Heptathlon, long jump (Seoul 1988), Heptathlon (Barcelona 1992)
SILVER (1): Heptathlon (Los Angeles 1984)
BRONZE (2): Long jump (Barcelona 1992), Long jump (Atlanta 1996)
TOTAL MEDALS:

CARL LEWIS

Carl Lewis is one of only six people to have won Olympic gold in the same event four times in a row – yet his long jump feats from 1984 in Los Angeles to Atlanta 12 years later are only part of his phenomenal story. He won 10 Olympics medals in all, nine of them gold – including one which was upgraded from silver when Canada's Ben Johnson was infamously disqualified after the 100m final at Seoul 1988 upon failing a drugs test. Lewis's four golds in Los Angeles in 1984 matched the tally of compatriot Jesse Owens at the Munich Olympics in 1936, and in the same four events – the 100m, 200m, 4 x 100m and long jump. Lewis was so confident that his first attempt in that summer's long jump final, measuring 8.54m, would be enough to win gold that after a foul in his next try he chose not to make any more – saving himself for the 200m and 4 x 100m races to come. Only swimmer Michael Phelps has more Olympic gold medals than the nine won by Lewis as well as Finnish runner Paavo Nurmi, Soviet gymnast Larisa Latynina and US swimmer Mark Spitz. Lewis has part-credited his late-career success to becoming a vegan in 1990.

BOB MATHIAS

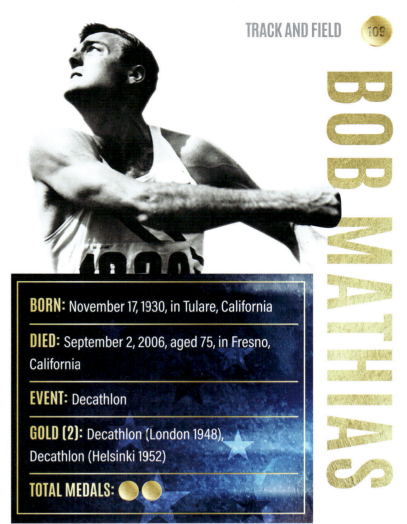

Bob Mathias was just 17 when he won Olympic gold in the decathlon at the 1948 Games in London, having only taken up the discipline earlier that year on the advice of his high school coach Virgil Jackson in Tulare, California. His lack of experience perhaps showed when he committed two fouls in the shot put event, unaware he was not meant to leave the throwing circle. But his finishing time of 5:11.00 in the final event, the 1500m, was enough to clinch gold – after a second day of competing that dragged on so late into the night that cars were driven in to Wembley Stadium with their headlights switched on to help. He responded to a question about how he would celebrate by suggesting: "I'll start shaving, I guess." Four years later in Helsinki he became the first decathlete to successfully defend his Olympic gold, ahead of compatriots Milton Campbell in second and Floyd Simmons third – a feat later matched by Great Britain's Daley Thompson. Mathias served as a Republican member of the US Congress between 1967 and 1975, having also worked as an actor in films including a 1954 biopic *The Bob Mathias Story*. He died of throat cancer in September 2006, aged 75.

BORN: November 17, 1930, in Tulare, California

DIED: September 2, 2006, aged 75, in Fresno, California

EVENT: Decathlon

GOLD (2): Decathlon (London 1948), Decathlon (Helsinki 1952)

TOTAL MEDALS: 🥇🥇

RIGHT: A poster promoting the 1948 London Olympics

BORN: July 1, 1961, in Birmingham, Alabama

EVENTS: 100, 200m, long jump

GOLD (9): 100m, 200m, 4 x 100m, long jump (Los Angeles 1984), 100m, long jump (Seoul 1988), 4 x 100m, long jump (Barcelona 1992), Long jump (Atlanta 1996)

SILVER (1): 200m (Seoul 1988)

TOTAL MEDALS: 🥇🥇🥇🥇🥇🥇🥇🥇🥇🥈

BOBBY MORROW

Bobby Morrow insisted on getting 11 hours sleep every night and joked he was "so perfectly relaxed that I can feel my jaw muscles wiggle". The sprinter who grew up on a cotton and carrot farm in Texas came back from the Melbourne Olympics in 1956 as the first person since Jesse Owens in 1936 to win both the 100m and 200m, adding 4 x 100m relay gold for good measure. He overtook compatriot Thane Baker halfway through the 100m final before cruising to victory, though they were both on the same side in the relay final alongside Ira Murchison and Leamon King – with Morrow running the final leg, finishing in a world record time of 39.5 seconds ahead of their USSR rivals in second. Morrow also set an Olympic record when winning the 200m final in 20.6 seconds, where the US dominated the podium with Andrew Stanfield taking silver and Baker bronze. Morrow attempted to qualify for a place on the US team at the 1960 Olympics in Rome but was unsuccessful in trials. He later worked in banking before his death from natural causes, at the age of 84, in May 2020.

BORN: October 15, 1935, in Harlingen, Texas
DIED: May 30, 2020, aged 84, in San Benito, Texas
EVENTS: 100m, 200m
GOLD (3): 100m, 200m, 4 x 100m (Melbourne 1956)
TOTAL MEDALS: 🥇🥇🥇

RIGHT: 1956 Melbourne Olympics advertising poster

EDWIN MOSES

Edwin Moses dominated the 400m hurdles for a decade, going 122 races unbeaten between 1977 and 1987 – while also winning Olympic gold in both Montreal in 1976 and Los Angeles in 1984, with only the USA's boycott of the 1980 Moscow Games denying him a shot at another medal in between. His huge running stride meant he typically covered the course in just 13 steps between hurdles rather than the more commonplace 14 or 15. The 1.85m-tall Moses won his first Olympic 400m hurdles gold in a world record time of 47.64 seconds in Montreal, just one of four world records he would set over the distance – and his victory by 8m was the biggest winning margin in the event's Olympics history. His fastest ever final was actually in Seoul in 1988, although that time his 47.56 seconds proved only enough to add a bronze medal to his previous achievements – finishing behind US team-mate Andre Phillips in first and Senegal's Amadou Dia bâ second. Since retirement Moses has worked as a sporting official toughening up anti-drug policies while also chairing since 2000 the Laureus World Sports Academy which aims to boost participation in sport while also promoting "social change". Moses was only the second man to win three 400m hurdles Olympics medals, after fellow American Morgan Taylor's gold at Paris 1924 and bronzes at Amsterdam 1928 and Los Angeles 1932.

BORN: August 31, 1955, in Dayton, Ohio
EVENT: 400m hurdles
GOLD (2): 400m hurdles (Montreal 1976), 400m hurdles (Los Angeles 1984)
BRONZE (1): 400m hurdles (Seoul 1988)
TOTAL MEDALS:

TRACK AND FIELD

PARRY O'BRIEN

BORN: January 28, 1932, in Santa Monica, California

DIED: April 21, 2007, aged 75, in Santa Clarita, California

EVENT: Shot put

GOLD (2): Shot put (Helsinki 1952), Shot put (Melbourne 1956)

SILVER (1): Shot put (Rome 1960)

TOTAL MEDALS: 🥇🥇🥈

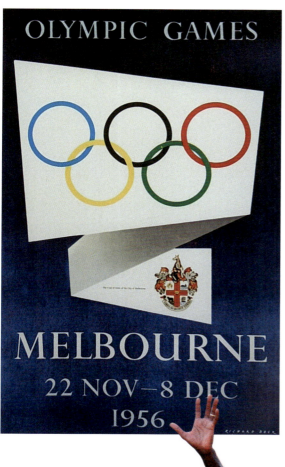

Parry O'Brien pioneered a new approach to the shot put which not only influenced others but helped him to dominate the event in the 1950s, including consecutive Olympic gold medal triumphs at the 1952 Games in Helsinki and in Melbourne four years later – although he had to settle only for silver at Rome 1960 in a surprise setback. O'Brien's style was to start by facing the back of the throwing circle, generating momentum with a 180-degrees spin before launching the shot – whereas fellow competitors had tended to stand face-forward and rock back on one foot before propelling it. O'Brien set shot put world records 17 times and was the first man to retain the event's Olympic title since another American, Ralph Rose, won the gold at St Louis in 1904 and in London four years later. O'Brien was given the honour of carrying the US flag at the Tokyo 1964 Olympics' opening ceremony – and was still competing in over-35s athletic events in 1984 at the age of 52, when he threw the shot 17.72m. His Olympic winning distances were 17.41m in 1952 and 18.51m in 1956 – the latter effort a whole 31cm ahead of silver medallist compatriot William Nieder, whereas his winning margin in 1952 was just 2cm ahead of the USA's Darrow Hooper.

ABOVE: Edwin Moses wins the gold medal in the Men's 400 metres hurdles, 1984 Summer Olympics in Los Angeles

AL OERTER

Al Oerter's discus triumph in Mexico City in 1968 made him the first person to win Olympics track and field gold in the same event four times in a row – his first coming as a 19-year-old in Melbourne 12 years earlier. His feat was only next matched by Carl Lewis, in the long jump, at the Atlanta Games in 1996. The year after his Olympics breakthrough Oerter almost died in a car crash but recovered sufficiently to retain his title in Rome in 1960, throwing an Olympic record of 59.18m – and he would set another Olympic best of 64.78m in Mexico City. Oerter's 1964 victory came despite a neck injury which had him wearing a brace not long before taking part and a torn rib cartilage he suffered while practicing a week before the event. He kept up his Olympics attendance after retiring from competing, carrying the US flag at the 1984 Games' opening ceremony in Los Angeles and bearing the Olympic torch into Atlanta's Centennial Olympic Stadium at the start of the event 12 years later. Oerter only took up the discus after one landed at his feet while he was sprinting on a track as a 15-year-old and he impressed a coach with the way he hurled it back.

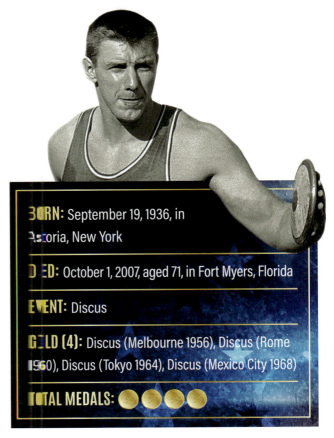

BORN: September 19, 1936, in Astoria, New York

DIED: October 1, 2007, aged 71, in Fort Myers, Florida

EVENT: Discus

GOLD (4): Discus (Melbourne 1956), Discus (Rome 1960), Discus (Tokyo 1964), Discus (Mexico City 1968)

TOTAL MEDALS: 🥇🥇🥇🥇

JESSE OWENS

Germany's Nazi dictator Adolf Hitler declared the 1936 Olympics in Berlin open, hoping it would promote "Aryan supremacy". But to his chagrin it was the USA's black athlete Jesse Owens who was the star of the Games, winning four gold track and field medals – in the 100m, 200m, 4 x 100m and long jump. Owens, son of a sharecropper, won the 200m in a world record time of 20.7 seconds – while the relay team's finish of 39.80 seconds was another global best. He became friends with his German rival for the long jump title, Luz Long – whose silver medal-winning leap of 7.87m was bested by Owens' 8.06m – and remained in touch with Long's family after the German's death during the Second World War's Battle of St Pietro in Italy in June 1943. Owens had been born with the first names James Cleveland but a schoolmistress misheard his initials J.C. and her mistaken version stuck. Despite his triumphs in Berlin, Owens was stripped of his amateur status by US officials after returning to America to discuss commercial sportswear deals rather than go on a post-Games tour of Sweden with team-mates. He suffered racial discrimination, struggled to find work and often had to take menial jobs, while also taking part in stunt races for cash – including against motorbikes, cars and horses. Owens died of lung cancer in March 1980, aged 66.

BORN: September 12, 1913, in Oakville, Alabama

DIED: March 31, 1980, aged 66, in Tucson, Arizona

EVENTS: 100m, 200m, long jump

GOLD (4): 100m, 200m, 4 x 100m, long jump (Berlin 1936)

TOTAL MEDALS: 🥇🥇🥇🥇

TRACK AND FIELD

BOB RICHARDS

Theology professor Bob Richards became known as the "Vaulting Vicar" as he followed up pole vault bronze in London in 1948, with golds in both Helsinki four years later and in Melbourne in 1952 – the only man to achieve that double. He also took part in the 1956 decathlon, finishing 13th. Richards had become ordained as a minister in 1946 and among his congregation members was future world tennis number one and six-time Wimbledon women's singles champion Billie Jean King. Richards clinched the 1952 gold by clearing 4.55m, ahead of compatriot Don Laz's 4.5m, then retained his title in Melbourne with a best of 4.56m – an Olympic record, for the second Games in succession, though he later confessed he was worried while lying in the pit that the bar he hit on his way over would topple. It did wobble, but stayed put, and another gold was his. Richards became the promotional "face" of Wheaties breakfast cereal, following on from other sporting stars such as baseball player Lou Gehrig and four-time 1936 Olympics gold medallist Jesse Owens. Richards later stood in the 1984 US presidential election, for the right-wing Populist Party, winning 62,646 votes. He died six days after turning 97 in February 2023.

BORN: February 20, 1926, in Champaign, Illinois
DIED: February 26, 2023, aged 97, in Waco, Texas
EVENTS: Pole vault, decathlon
GOLD (2): Pole vault (Helsinki 1952), Pole vault (Melbourne 1956)
BRONZE (1): Pole vault (London 1948)
TOTAL MEDALS:

ABOVE: The official poster of the Berlin 1936 Games, which depicts an athlete and the Brandenburg Gate

RALPH ROSE

Six-time Olympic medallist Ralph Rose, 197cm-tall and weighing in at 115kg, dominated the shot put across three Olympics in 1904, 1908 and 1912 – taking three golds, including being the first and only person to win the two handed shot put event which was only ever held in Stockholm in 1912. In between he set a world record in 1909, throwing the 16lb ball 15.5m – a distance not bettered for another 16 years. Rose also carried the US flag at the opening ceremony of the 1908 Olympics in London, though he is said to have offended the British hosts by failing to dip it towards White City Stadium's royal box as athletes from other nations had. The other six finalists to complete their shot put attempts in St Louis in 1904 were all also American – Greece's Nikolaos Georgantas pulled out in disgust after his first two efforts were disallowed. Rose's compatriot Martin Sheridan beat him to gold in that summer's discus in a final throw-off, after the pair initially tied with best distances of 39.28m. Rose died of pneumonia aged just 28 in October 1913.

BORN: March 17, 1885, in Healdsburg, California

DIED: October 16, 1913, aged 28, in San Francisco, California

EVENTS: Discus, hammer, shot put

GOLD (3): Shot put (St Louis 1904), Shot put (London 1908), Two handed shot put (Stockholm 1912)

SILVER (2): Discus (St Louis 1904), Shot put (Stockholm 1912)

BRONZE (1): Hammer (St Louis 1904)

TOTAL MEDALS: 🥇🥇🥇🥈🥈🥉

WILMA RUDOLPH

Wilma Rudolph weighed just 2kg when born prematurely in June 1940, the 20th of her father Ed's 22 children, and lost the use of her left leg during childhood while suffering from not only polio but also pneumonia and scarlet fever. Yet despite having to wear a leg brace until the age of 12, she staged a recovery helped by daily massages from family members and weekly treatment at Meharry Medical College in Nashville, Tennessee, some 80km from her Clarksville home. She went from wearing a brace to donning an orthopaedic shoe but was able to discard this and play basketball barefoot with her brothers, before showing talent on the track at high school. Rudolph was just 16, the youngest member of the US team, when she ran the third leg to help win 4 x 100m bronze at the 1956 Olympics in Melbourne. Four years later in Rome she surged to a hat-trick of golds in the 100m, 200m and 4 x 100m – emulating what Australia's Betty Cuthbert had done in Melbourne. Rudolph, the first American woman to win three golds at a single Games, retired from sport after Rome 1960 and later worked as a teacher and coach before dying of brain cancer aged 54 in November 1994.

MEL SHEPPARD

Melvin Sheppard was once rejected when he applied to join the New York Police and was told this was because he had an enlarged and weak heart. Yet that appeared no obstacle to him winning three gold medals at the London Olympics in 1908 and another in Stockholm four years later. His first was in the 1500m in London, where he overtook Great Britain's Harold Wilson 15 yards from the finishing line, before keeping the lead from 500m onwards in the 800m final ahead of Italy's Emilio Lunghi. He then ran the fourth and final leg as the US won the medley relay, which involved two athletes running 200m each then a third covering 400m and a fourth 800m – and with athletes touching hands at the changeovers rather than handing over batons. This was the first ever relay final at the Olympics, though also the first and last time it was run in this medley format. Sheppard then ran the first leg in the 4 x 400m final in Stockholm, where the US team – also comprising Edward Lindberg, Ted Meredith and Charles Reidpath – won in a world record time of 3:16.6.

BORN: September 5, 1883, in Almonesson, New Jersey

DIED: January 4, 1942, aged 58, in Queens, New York

EVENTS: 400m, 800m, 1500m

GOLD (4): 800m, 1500m, medley relay (London 1908), 4 x 400m (Stockholm 1912)

SILVER (1): 800m (Stockholm 1912)

TOTAL MEDALS: 🥇🥇🥇🥇🥈

BORN: June 23, 1940, in Saint Bethlehem, Tennessee

DIED: November 12, 1994, aged 54, in Brentwood, Tennessee

EVENTS: 100m, 200m

GOLD (3): 100m, 200m, 4 x 100m (Rome 1960)

BRONZE (1): 4 x 100m (Melbourne 1956)

TOTAL MEDALS: 🥇🥇🥇🥉

RIGHT: 1960 Rome Olympic Games poster

TOMMIE SMITH

Tommie Smith, along with team-mate John Carlos and white Australian athlete Peter Norman, carried out one of the most striking gestures in Olympics history when the US pair raised black-gloved fists on the winning podium in Mexico City in 1968 as a "Black Power" statement against racial injustice. Smith was receiving his gold medal for winning the men's 200m final in a world record 19.83 seconds, and was joined in the salute by bronze medallist Carlos while second-placed Norman wore a civil rights badge they gave him. Smith later said they were "just human beings who saw a need to bring attention to the inequality in our country", adding: "There was nothing but a raised fist in the air and a bowed head, acknowledging the American flag – not symbolising a hatred for it." Smith and Carlos were pallbearers at Norman's funeral in 2006 after the Australian's death aged 64. Smith's 1968 Mexico City race was the first 200m run officially recorded at under 20 seconds – and he was so clear of the field he raised his arms in triumph 10m from the finishing line. He later played NFL football for the Cincinnati Bengals before working as a track coach and college teacher.

BORN: June 6, 1944, in Clarksville, Texas
EVENT: 200m
GOLD (1): 200m (Mexico City 1968)
TOTAL MEDALS: 🥇

JIM THORPE

Jim Thorpe was one of his names. Another given to him by his part-Native American parents was Wa-Tho-Huk, meaning "Bright Path". After his mother died when he was 12 and his father three years later, Thorpe impressed at a government-run school on the gridiron football field, but also in athletics – prompting his call-up for the 1912 Olympics in Stockholm. Thorpe won pentathlon gold in Sweden, finishing first in the 200m, 1500m, discus and long jump as well as third in javelin – prompting coaches to put him forward for the decathlon too, where he also won comfortably with a new world record of 8,413 points. He also finished fourth that summer in the high jump and seventh in the long jump. Sweden's King Gustaf V, handing over a bronze bust to Thorpe for his pentathlon triumph, told him: "Sir, you are the greatest athlete in the world." The winner replied: "Thanks, King." Thorpe was given a ticker-tape celebration in New York City on returning home to the US, only for his medals to be stripped from him the following year. His apparent offence was breaking amateur rules by playing semi-professional baseball. His gold medallist status was only officially restored in 1982, almost 30 years after his death following heart failure at the age of 65 in March 1953.

ABOVE: Jim Thorpe at the 1912 Summer Olympics

TRACK AND FIELD

WYOMIA TYUS

BORN: August 29, 1945, in Griffin, Georgia

EVENTS: 100m, 200m

GOLD (3): 100m (Tokyo 1964), 100m, 4 x 100m (Mexico City 1968)

SILVER (1): 4 x 100m (Tokyo 1964)

TOTAL MEDALS: 🥇🥇🥇🥈

BORN: May 28, 1888, in Bellemont, Oklahoma

DIED: March 28, 1953, aged 65, in Lomita, California

EVENTS: Decathlon, high jump, long jump, pentathlon

GOLD (2): Decathlon, pentathlon (Stockholm 1912)

TOTAL MEDALS: 🥇🥇

Five more people have done so since, but Wyomia Tyus was the first person to take Olympic gold in the 100m twice in a row. She followed up her Tokyo 1964 winning time of 11.4, 0.2 seconds ahead of compatriot Edith McGuire, by running a world record 11.08 in Mexico City four years later as a 23-year-old – though only on being given a second chance after a false start. Tyus and McGuire were fellow students at Tennessee State University and Tokyo was the first time Tyus finished in front of her longtime rival. Having helped the US team to 4 x 100m silver in Tokyo, Tyus went one better in that event in Mexico City – running the final leg to complete a new world record time of 42.88, shared with teammates Barbara Ferrell, Margaret Bailes and Mildrette Netter. Tyus also reached the 200m final in 1968, finishing sixth. Those who have followed in her speedy double 100m gold-winning footsteps are the USA's Carl Lewis and Jamaica's Usain Bolt in the men's event, fellow Americans Gail Devers and Jamaica's Shelly-Ann Fraser-Pryce and Elaine Thompson-Herah in the women's.

MAL WHITFIELD

Mal Whitfield's first Olympics was the 1932 Games – not as a competitor, but as a seven-year-old spectator who sneaked his way into the Los Angeles Memorial Coliseum. Just 16 years later the 23-year-old US Air Force sergeant was a double gold medallist at London 1948, adding another four years later in Helsinki.

Between those two Games he served as a tail-gunner during the Korean War, carrying out 27 bomber missions. Whitfield finished both the 1948 and 1952 800m finals in times of 1:49.2 seconds – and both times ahead of Jamaica's Arthur Wint who twice had to settle for silver. His 4 x 400m triumph in London, running the final leg, came alongside not only Arthur Harnden and Clifford Bourland but also Leroy Cochran whose elder brother Commodore helped win gold in the same event 24 years earlier in Paris. Wint was on the Jamaican team who gained revenge by winning gold in the 4 x 400m final in Helsinki in 1952, just ahead of Whitfield's US team. Whitfield later worked as a goodwill ambassador and international diplomat supporting sports scholarships for African athletes across the world. He is buried in Arlington National Cemetery, following his death aged 91 in November 2015.

BORN: October 11, 1924, in Bay City, Texas

DIED: November 19, 2015, aged 91, in Washington, D.C.

EVENTS: 400m, 800m

GOLD (3): 800m, 4 x 400m (London 1948), 800m (Helsinki 1952)

SILVER (1): 4 x 400m (Helsinki 1952)

BRONZE (1): 400m (London 1948)

TOTAL MEDALS: 🥇🥇🥇🥈🥉

LAURYN WILLIAMS

Lauryn Williams is the only American woman – and one of just six people – to have won medals at both the Summer and Winter Olympics. She sprinted to silver aged 20 in the 100m final at the 2004 games in Athens, only just beaten at the last by Belarus's Yuliya Nesterenko in 10.93 seconds to Williams' 10.96. Williams went on to win gold at London 2012, having anchored the US team to victory in their heat before Tianna Madison, Allyson Felix, Bianca Knight and Carmelita Jeter triumphed in the final. After switching to bobsleigh she won Winter Olympics silver at the 2014 Games in Sochi in Russia, in the two-woman bobsleigh along with Elana Meyers – only ten hundredths of a second behind Canada's Kaillie Humphries and Heather Moyse. The other athletes to

BORN: September 11, 1983, in Rochester, Pennsylvania

EVENT: 100m

GOLD (1): 4 x 100m (London 2012)

SILVER (1): 100m (Athens 2004)

TOTAL MEDALS: 🥇🥈

BABE DIDRIKSON ZAHARIAS

Mildred "Babe" Didrikson became the Olympics' first women's 80m hurdles champion in Los Angeles in 1932, having already won gold in the javelin. Her throw set an Olympic record of 43.68m and her run – following a false start – a world record of 11.7 seconds although it had appeared a dead heat with compatriot Evelyne Hall who was given silver. Didrikson had trained as a youngster by leaping over neighbours' hedges she insisted be trimmed to the right Olympic height. She was also given joint share of the world record for the high jump at the 1932 Games, tying with US team-mate Jean Shiley on clearing 1.657m – but Shiley was awarded gold by judges who ruled Didrikson's attempt a foul as her head went over the bar before her body did. Didrikson later excelled at golf, winning 10 major championships and competed against men in the PGA's 1938 Los Angeles Open. She died from colon cancer in September 1956 aged 45. Her life story was told in a 1975 TV movie called *Babe*, with Susan Clark playing her. Clark's future husband Alex Karras played George Zaharias, a professional wrestler who married Didrikson in 1938 and was her manager during her golf career. The women's 80m hurdles was later changed to a 100m race at the 1972 Olympics in Munich.

BORN: June 26, 1911, in Port Arthur, Texas

DIED: September 27, 1956, aged 45, in Galveston, Texas

EVENTS: Discus, high jump, javelin, long jump, shot put

GOLD (2): 80m hurdles, javelin (Los Angeles 1932)

SILVER (1): High jump (Los Angeles 1932)

TOTAL MEDALS: 🥇🥇🥈

BELOW: Poster for the 1932 Los Angeles Olympic Games

win medals at both the Summer and Winter Olympics are the US's Eddie Eagan (boxing gold in 1920, four-man bobsleigh gold in 1932) and Eddy Alvarez (baseball silver in 2020, 5000m short track speed skating relay in 2014), Norway's Jacob Tullin Thams (8m sailing silver in 1936, ski jumping gold in 1924), East Germany's Christa Luding-Rothenburger (cycling sprint silver in 1988 as well as 500m speed skating gold in 1984, 1000m speed skating gold and 500m speed skating silver in 1988, and 500m speed skating bronze in 1992), and Canada's Clara Hughes who followed her two bronzes in the cycling road race and time trial in 1996 with 5000m speed skating bronze in 2002, team pursuit speed skating silver and 5000m speed skating gold four years later and 5000m speed skating bronze in 2010.

VOLLEYBALL

Indoor volleyball was played as a demonstration sport at the 1924 Olympics in Paris but was only added as a medal contest at the 1964 Games in Tokyo. Men's and women's tournaments have been held at every Olympics since. Beach volleyball, played on sand courts, made its Olympic debut as a demonstration sport in Barcelona in 1992 before becoming a medal event four years later. The Champ de Mars public green space overlooked by the Eiffel Tower in Paris was chosen to host the 2024 Olympics beach volleyball.

KARCH KIRALY

BORN: November 3, 1960, in Jackson, Michigan

EVENTS: Volleyball – indoor volleyball, beach volleyball

POSITION: Outside hitter

GOLD (3): Indoor volleyball (Los Angeles 1984), Indoor volleyball (Seoul 1988), Beach volleyball (Atlanta 1996)

TOTAL MEDALS: 🥇🥇🥇

Volleyball was invented by an American, William G. Morgan, in Massachusetts in 1895 – but it took another 20 years after it was introduced as an Olympic sport in 1964 for the US to first win a medal in either men's or women's indoor volleyball. That drought ended when the men won gold in Los Angeles in 1984, beating Brazil 15-6, 15-6, 15-7 in the final. On the team was Charles "Karch" Kiraly, who then captained the US as they retained gold four years later in Seoul. The passer/outside-hitter dubbed the "Thunderball in Volleyball" later became the first person to win Olympic gold in both indoor volleyball and beach volleyball, after the latter was added to the Games for the first time in Atlanta in 1996. Kiraly partnered with Kent Steffes to win gold in Atlanta, defeating fellow Americans Michael Dodd and Michael Whitmarsh 12-5, 12-8 in the final. He enjoyed even more Olympic glory 25 years later at Tokyo 2020, coaching the US women's team to indoor volleyball gold after their bronze at Rio 2016. On the day they defeated Brazil 3-0 in the Tokyo 2020 final, he revealed for the first time he was in remission after being diagnosed with colon cancer in 2017.

ABOVE: Karch Kiraly celebrates a point during a match versus the Canadian team of Heese/Child at the 1996 Atlanta Beach Centennial Olympic Games

MISTY MAY-TREANOR

Beach volleyball was introduced as an Olympic sport in 1996, differing from indoor volleyball by having just two rather than six players per side – and being played on courts made of sand. The US had to wait until Athens 2004 for their first women's beach volleyball gold medallists – but it was merely the first triumph of three in a row for the pair initially known as Misty May and Kerri Walsh. They had teamed up in 2001, a year after Walsh competed in the indoor volleyball and May in the beach volleyball at the Sydney Games. They won all seven games in 2004 without dropping a set, beating Brazil's Adriana Behar and Shelda Bede 21-17, 21-11 in the final. The team now using married names Misty May-Treanor and Kerri Walsh Jennings retained their title four years later in Beijing again without conceding a set, clinching gold 21-18, 20-18 against their Chinese hosts' Tian Jia and Wang Jie amid a downpour at Chaoyang Park Beach. The London 2012 tournament took place on Horse Guards Parade in central London, close by 10 Downing Street and Buckingham Palace. The same team reigned again, with May-Treanor and Walsh Jennings winning an all-American final against Jennifer Kessy and April Ross. May-Treanor's father Robert "Butch" May was previously part of the US men's indoor volleyball team at the 1968 Olympics in Mexico City, finishing seventh as the USSR won gold.

BELOW: Misty May-Treanor serving against Brazil in the 2008 Olympic quarter-final match

BORN: July 30, 1977, in Los Angeles, California

EVENT: Volleyball – beach volleyball

GOLD (3): Athens 2004, Beijing 2008, London 2012

TOTAL MEDALS: 🥇🥇🥇

KERRI WALSH JENNINGS

OLYMPIC LEGENDS USA

Records set by Olympics beach volleyball champion pair Misty May-Treanor and Kerri Walsh Jennings included an unprecedented 112-match winning streak in 2007 and 2008, beating their own previous best of 89. Their partnership came to an end when May-Treanor retired after that third Olympic title at London 2012, a triumph which came despite Walsh Jennings being five weeks pregnant with her third child. After giving birth to daughter Scout in April 2013, Walsh Jennings later returned to beach volleyball with new playing partner April Ross – one of her defeated opponents that 2012 summer in England. They qualified together for the 2016 Summer Olympics in Rio. This time the US pair had to settle for bronze, after a 22-20, 21-18 semi-final defeat to Brazil's Ágatha Bednarczuk and Bárbara Seixas in a temporary stadium on Copacabana Beach. They recovered to beat another host nation pair Talita Antunes and Larissa França 17-21, 21-17, 15-9 for a place on the podium. That made Walsh Jennings the beach volleyball player with more Olympic medals than any other – but she and new partner Brooke Sweat were unable to make it through US qualifiers to take part at Tokyo 2020.

BORN: August 16, 1978, in Santa Clara, California

EVENT: Volleyball – beach volleyball

GOLD (3): Athens 2004, Beijing 2008, London 2012

BRONZE (1): Rio 2016

TOTAL MEDALS: 🥇🥇🥇🥉

BELOW: Kerri Walsh Jennings (left) celebrates with teammate Misty May-Treanor (right) after winning the Women's Gold Medal Match vs China at the 2008 Beijing Olympic Games

LEFT: Kerri Walsh Jennings looks on during the Women's Beach Volleyball Gold medal match against the United States on Day 12 of the London 2012 Olympic Games

WRESTLING

Martial arts and combat sports at the Olympics include not only boxing, but also fencing, judo, taekwondo and wrestling. There are two different wrestling disciplines, fought at different weights: freestyle and Greco-Roman. The only modern Olympics not to feature any wrestling was the 1900 Games in Paris. The International Olympic Committee did vote in 2013 to drop wrestling from the Games but the sport was reprieved after protests. Women's events were introduced at the 2004 Olympics in Athens.

DAN GABLE

Munich 1972 gold medal winner Dan Gable has gone down as one of freestyle wrestling's most-admired and successful competitors – and coaches. He was a fierce trainer, with one pastime being to turn over each card in a pack and do as many press-ups as each number suggested – seeing how many times he could go through the deck. As a youngster, even when mowing the lawn he would do so while jogging, wearing a rubber suit and burdened further by arm and leg weights. His dedication paid off when he finished top of the freestyle 68kg standings at the 1972 Games, after accumulating the fewest penalty points in his bouts. The scoring system was changed in 1984 to prioritise positive points, awarded for moves such as holds, actions and near-throws. Freestyle wrestling allows fighters to use legs in both attack and defence, unlike Greco-Roman wrestling which also bars combatants from holds below the waist. Gable won 299 matches between 1963 and 1973 – including all six in Munich – while losing only six and drawing three. Three of his 1972 Olympics victories were achieved by a fall – that is, pinning both opponents' shoulders to the mat, adding four penalty points to their overall score and none to his. Gable later became a successful coach, training 12 Olympians including eight medallists.

BELOW: Dan Gable in action versus Yugoslavian Safer Sali during the Lightweight (68kg) Round 1 match at the 1972 Summer Olympics

BORN: October 25, 1948, in Waterloo, Iowa

EVENTS: Wrestling - freestyle

GOLD (1): Freestyle 68kg (Munich 1972)

TOTAL MEDALS: 🥇

RULON GARDNER

US Greco-Roman wrestler Rulon Gardner pulled off a major shock at the 2000 Sydney Olympics. He went into the 130kg final with most expecting Russia's Aleksandr Karelin to win gold for the fourth Games in a row, having not lost a match since 1987 and won 59 Olympics bouts with no defeats. Yet Gardner, 29, prevailed after three rounds. What proved to be the decisive moment came in the second, when Karelin's hands slipped apart while they had their arms wrapped around each other in a clinch – he was penalised, with a point awarded to his opponent. Gardner, who attributes his physical strength to growing up and working hard on a dairy farm in Iowa, added bronze in Athens four years later. But his preparations had been less than ideal – he lost the middle toe of his right foot to frostbite, after crashing his snowmobile into Wyoming's freezing Salt River in February 2002 and being left stranded for 18 hours, then the following year was in a motorbike crash. His final wrestling match was at Athens 2004, where he beat Iran's Sajjad Barzi 3-0 in the bronze medal match and signalled his retirement by following the tradition of leaving his shoes in the middle of the mat.

LEFT: Gardner (right) competing at the 2004 Olympic Games in Athens

BORN: August 16, 1971, in Afton, Wyoming

EVENT: Wrestling – Greco-Roman

GOLD (1): Greco-Roman 130kg (Sydney 2000)

BRONZE (1): Greco-Roman 120kg (Athens 2004)

TOTAL MEDALS:

OLYMPIC LEGENDS FROM THE REST OF THE WORLD

Going into the 2024 Olympics in Paris, the United States was clearly leader at the top of the overall medals table – with 2,629 including 1,061 golds, ahead of the former USSR in second on 1,010. Yet many of the most impressive, successful and fondly recalled Olympic performers have come from other nations all across the world. Six countries have provided competitors at all 29 Summer Olympics: Australia, France, Great Britain, Greece, Italy and Switzerland.

KENENISA BEKELE

Ethiopian Haile Gebrselassie won Olympic gold in the 10,000m at both the 1996 Olympics in Atlanta and the follow-up four years later in Sydney – a double that was then emulated by his compatriot Kenenisa Bekele in Athens in 2004, where Gebrselassie finished fifth, and at Beijing 2008 where the former champion this time came in sixth. Another Ethiopian, Sileshi Sihine, took silver behind Bekele in both Athens and Beijing – in Athens the pair waited for Gebrselassie to cross the finishing line before sharing a lap of honour with him. Both Bekele's victories came in Olympic record times – 27:05.10 in 2004, 27:01.17 in 2008. He also won 5,000m silver in 2004 then gold four years later, as well as five World Athletics Championships golds between 2003 and 2009. These included his victory in the 10,000m final in Helsinki in 2005 just months after Bekele's fiancée Alem Techale died of a heart attack, aged only 18, while doing a training run with him. Bekele held the 10,000m world record of 26:17.53 for 15 years until it was bettered by Uganda's Joshua Cheptegei, running 26:11.00 in October 2020 a year before he won 10,000m silver and 5,000m gold at the delayed Tokyo 2020 Games. Cheptegei had previously beaten Bekele's 5,000m world record of 12:37.35, taking it down to 12:35.36.

FANNY BLANKERS-KOEN

"The Flying Housewife" Francina "Fanny" Blankers-Koen was the unexpected star of the 1948 Olympics in London – having been written off by many as too old at 30 and as a mother-of-two. Yet she surged to 100m gold in 11.9 seconds before adding three more triumphs – in the 80m hurdles, in an Olympic record 11.2 seconds, the 200m and as the anchor in the 4 x 100m relay when she recovered from third place on the final leg to finish first. Blankers-Koen's 80m hurdles victory was declared after a photo finish alongside Great Britain's Maureen Gardner though she initially thought she had lost because a band inside Wembley Stadium began playing the UK national anthem. It transpired this was merely because the British royal family had arrived at that precise moment. Blankers-Koen previously competed at the 1936 Olympics in Berlin as an 18-year-old finishing fifth in both the high jump and the 4 x 100m relay – while also getting the autograph of the USA's four-time gold medallist Jesse Owens, something she would treasure and from someone she would go on to emulate. The International Association of Athletics Federations honoured her in 1999 as the "Female Athlete of the Century", five years before her death aged 85 in January 2004 after suffering with Alzheimer's disease.

OLYMPIC LEGENDS FROM THE REST OF THE WORLD

USAIN BOLT

Usain Bolt really did electrify athletics like the lightning bolt he would mimic in his celebratory poses on the track – of which there have been many. In 2008 in Beijing he became the first man since Carl Lewis in Los Angeles in 1984 to win both 100m and 200m Olympic gold, but the manner of his victories proved just as captivating. In the Bird's Nest Stadium he set new world records in both events. He finished in 9.69 seconds in the 100m despite a slow start, with his left foot trainer unlaced and while easing up to begin celebrating with 15m still to go, and ran the 200m in 19.30. He also helped Jamaica win 4 x 100m gold though this title was rescinded nine years later after team-mate Nesta Carter was found guilty of taking a banned substance. In 2009 Bolt set a new 100m best of 9.58 at the World Athletics Championship in Berlin – a world record which still stands, as does his 19.19 in the 200m at that same tournament. Bolt, who often joked about living on a diet of McDonald's chicken nuggets, retained his individual titles at London 2012 and Beijing 2016 as well as adding 4 x 100m golds both times. Bolt's London 2012 winning times were 9.63 seconds in the 100m and 19.32 in the 200m, which he followed up in Rio by running 9.81 and 19.78.

NADIA COMĂNECI

No gymnast had ever been awarded a perfect score of 10 out of 10 by judges at an Olympic Games, until Romania's Nadia Comăneci managed it not just once in Montreal in 1976 but seven times. The Romanian 14-year-old won three golds that summer, in the all-round, uneven bars and balance beam individual events – before adding another two in Moscow four years later, in the balance beam and floor exercise disciplines. The USSR's Nellie Kim, who won silver to Comăneci's gold in the 1976 all-around final, was given two 10.0 scores that summer – in the uneven bars and the balance beam. Four of Comăneci's top scores came for her athletic, graceful and speedy performances on the uneven bars, three on the balance beam. Such a performance was so unexpected, the electronic scoreboards were not programmed to display a perfect 10 – instead first showing her mark from the judges as 1.00. She remains the youngest Olympic all-around champion, with the rules now stipulating competitors must turn 16 in the same calendar year as their Games. Comăneci defected from Communist Romania to the United States in November 1989 and became a US citizen 12 years later. In 1996 she married Bart Conner, a former gymnast who won team and parallel bars gold medals for the US at the 1984 Los Angeles Olympics.

MO FARAH

Mohamed Farah was born in what is now Somalia, with the name Hussein Abdi Kahin, before being trafficked to England aged nine under the name he would adopt before going on to become Great Britain's most successful Olympics track athlete. Farah won his first Olympics gold in the 10,000m in London's Olympic Stadium in 2012, timing his surge through the field perfectly to eventually cruise over the line in a time of 27:30.42. That made him Team GB's third athletics gold medallist that day, on what would quickly be dubbed Britain's "Super Saturday", after triumphs for team-mates Jessica Ennis in the heptathlon and, more unexpectedly, Greg Rutherford in the long jump. Farah added 5,000m gold in similar style a week later – in a time of 13:41.66. He then retained both titles at the Rio 2016 Olympics, triumphantly running the 10,000m in 27:05.17, just about edging past Kenya's Paul Tanui – despite Farah being accidentally clipped by training partner Galen Rupp and falling on the tenth lap – and the 5,000m in 13:03.30. The only other man to win the 5,000m and the 10,000m at two different Olympics was Finland's Lasse Virén at Munich 1972 and Montreal 1976. Farah – who would celebrate by using his hands above his head to form an M-shape, a move called the "Mobot" – was made a Sir by the late Queen Elizabeth II in 2017.

BIRGIT FISCHER

Birgit Fischer is the most successful Olympics kayaker, winning eight golds and 12 medals overall across seven Games representing first East Germany and then Germany following reunification. Her first Olympic title came aged 18, her latest at the age of 42 in Athens in 2004 – having twice come out of retirement, vowing to quit after both the 1988 and 2000 Games but later changing her mind. Her former husband Jörg Schmidt won silver for East Germany at the 1988 Seoul Olympics, in the men's C-1 1000m race in a summer which saw his wife capture not only a silver of her own but also two golds. Her niece Fanny Fischer won gold in the women's K-4 500m race at the 2008 Olympics in Beijing, an event Birgit won in Atlanta in 1996 and in Athens four years before Fanny's success. Birgit also won 38 ICF Canoe Sprint World Championships medals, including 28 golds, while her brother Frank won nine – four of his being gold. Her triumph in the K-2 500m final at Sydney 2000, alongside Katrin Wagner, made her the first woman to win at least two medals at four different Olympics – having already won gold with Wagner, Manuela Mücke and Anett Schuck in the K-4 500m that summer.

ALADÁR GEREVICH

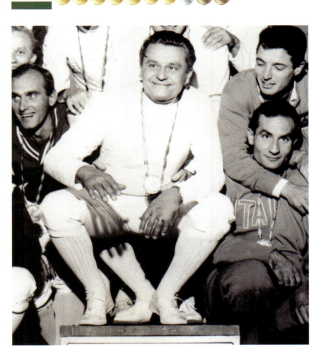

Aladár Gerevich has been labelled "the greatest Olympic swordsman ever" and few could disagree, simply looking at his record of seven Olympic golds stretching across an amazing 28-year reign from the 1932 Games in Los Angeles to the 1960 event in Rome. He would surely have won even more had the Second World War not meant there were no Olympics in 1940 nor 1944. All his golds came in the sabre team event, except for his individual triumph at the 1948 Olympics in London where he won all seven of his contests – two more than Italy's Vincenzo Pinton. Hungarian teams won gold in eight of the first ten team sabre Olympic events up to 1960, where Gerevich bowed out with his last victory at the age of 50, but their most recent since then was in Seoul in 1988. Hungary took bronze in the men's team sabre at Tokyo 2020, behind gold medallists South Korea and silver-winning Italy, while the women's event that summer was won by a Russian Olympic Committee team, followed by France in second and South Korea third. Gerevich's wife Erna Bogen won fencing bronze at the 1932 Olympics in Los Angeles, in the women's individual foil – 20 years after her father won team sabre silver for Austria at the 1912 Games in Stockholm. Aladár and Erna's son Pál Gerevich went on to win bronze in the team sabre at Munich 1972 and Moscow 1980.

CHRIS HOY

The hosts Great Britain – now branded as Team GB – won 65 medals at the London 2012 Olympics, their biggest tally since the 146 claimed in the same city back in 1908, though they would go on to take 67 at Rio 2016. Among the major winners at London 2012 was cyclist Chris Hoy, from the Scottish capital Edinburgh. His two golds in the team sprint and Keirin races made him the first British competitor to have won six Olympic titles, one more than rower Steve Redgrave. His first had come in Athens in 2004, in the 1km "kilo" time trial – the last time that event was part of the Olympics. Four years later he added another three golds in Beijing, the first Briton to win as many at a single Games for a century, and in 2012 he was Team GB's flag-carrier at the opening ceremony in London's Olympic Stadium before his team sprint triumph alongside Jason Kenny and Philip Hindes and his individual win in the Keirin. He retired in 2013, having said in the immediate aftermath of his London 2012 glory that there was only a "0.01 per cent chance" of targeting Rio 2016. He also vowed to down plenty of celebratory beers, ending four years of abstinence – telling reporters: "I'll definitely be making up for my lost units." He had been knighted in 2009, making him Sir Chris Hoy.

SAWAO KATŌ

No male gymnast has won more Olympic golds than Japan's Sawao Katō, who clinched eight across the Mexico City 1968, Munich 1972 and Montreal 1976 Games – while only three men have more gymnastics medals overall: Russia's Nikolai Andrianov on 15, his compatriot Boris Shakhlin two further back and Japan's Takashi Ono also with 13. Kato, standing at just 1.63m but with superb composure, became in 1976 the first man to successfully defend the parallel bars title. Katō's brother Takeshi, four years older, won team gold alongside him in Mexico City as well as bronze in the floor exercise. The younger brother's team gold in Montreal four years later was a painful ordeal for Japanese colleague Shun Fujimoto, who broke his leg at the knee during his floor exercise routine but went ahead with the side horse exercise and dislocated his knee further in the dismount – but did enough to help Japan win gold with an overall score of 576.85, ahead of the USSR's 576.45. Katō later served as head judge for the gymnastics at the 2004 Olympics in Athens.

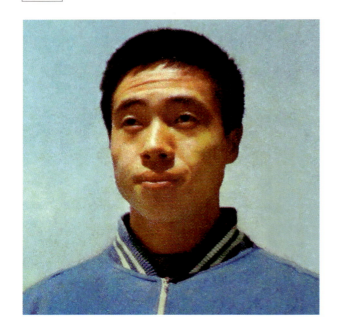

JASON KENNY

Jason Kenny, then 20, was beaten by Great Britain teammate Chris Hoy in the Beijing 2008 final of the cycling sprint – which since 2004 challenges the two cyclists to ride for 750m, though only really racing for the last 200m. The pair were both gold medallists on the same side in that summer's team sprint event. Kenny has since gone on to overtake Hoy as Britain's most successful Olympian, with more medals than anyone else – nine – as well as most golds, seven. His latest came in the Keirin at Tokyo 2020, where he surged clear of Malaysia's Azizulhasni to successfully defend the title he won at Rio 2016 – just as he had repeated Olympic gold in the team sprint in 2008, 2012 and 2016 and the individual sprint in 2012 and 2016. After his Tokyo 2020 success he was knighted, while his fellow cyclist wife Laura Kenny – née Trott – was made a Dame.

LARISA LATYNINA

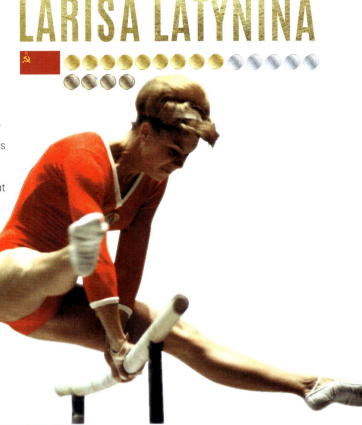

Only US swimmer Michael Phelps, with 23, has more Olympic gold medals than Larisa Latynina's nine – while her 18 medals overall put her ahead of all other gymnasts. She made her Games debut as a 21-year-old in Melbourne in 1956, where she clinched her first four golds – in the all-around, floor exercise, team and vault finals. She was still winning multiple medals in Tokyo eight years later, two golds and a bronze, to go with not only her Olympic medals but also 14 from the Artistic Gymnastics World Championships (nine gold) and another 14 from the European Women's Gymnastic Championships (seven gold). Latynina, born in what is now Ukraine, lost both parents in the aftermath of the Second World War. She took up gymnastics as an 11-year-old, impressing school teachers with her skills doing exercises with balls and hoops. Latynina later said: "I repeat my old routine hundreds, sometimes thousands of times. Monotonous? Not at all." After retiring as a competitor she became coach of the USSR's Olympics team, helping guide them to golds at the Mexico City 1968, Munich 1972 and Montreal 1976 Olympics.

PAAVO NURMI

The "Flying Finn" Paavo Nurmi ruled the world when it came to middle- and long-distance running through the 1920s, winning nine Olympic golds and three silvers at Antwerp 1920, Paris 1924 and Amsterdam 1928 – while still feeling annoyed his country failed to enter him for the 10,000m in Paris, an event he remained unbeaten in elsewhere. One protest by Nurmi did work out – he was upset to discover in Paris that there was only 30 minutes between the men's 1500m and 5,000m events, but he and Finland's officials managed to get the gap widened to two hours. But he was denied his hope of running the marathon at the 1932 Olympics in Los Angeles after having his amateur status questioned. Nurmi, who would often run clutching a stopwatch in his hands, later ran into the host stadium carrying the Olympic torch when his homeland hosted the 1952 Summer Games in the country's capital Helsinki. Nurmi, who set 22 world records during his running career, later worked an athletics coach and successful businessman before dying aged 76 in October 1973, prompting Finland to grant him a state funeral where six of his country's other gold medallists were pallbearers. Nurmi was the running hero of Hollywood actor Dustin Hoffman's character in the 1976 movie *Marathon Man*.

LÁSZLÓ PAPP

László Papp was the first boxer to win gold at three consecutive Olympics, first in the middleweight category at London 1948 before moving into the light middleweight events at the two Summer Games which followed – triumphing in all 13 of his matches and only dropping one round, in the 1956 final he nevertheless went on to win against future world light heavyweight champion José Torres. Papp's first Olympic victory in London was against the home favourite, Great Britain's John Wright. Papp's dominance was despite his height being a mere 1.65m and he went through his entire career undefeated – winning 27 times and drawing twice. As well as being a triple Olympic gold medallist, he also won the European Amateur Championships as a middleweight in 1949 and as a light middleweight two years later. The Hungarian government allowed him to fight professionally, the first boxer from a Communist country given such permission, yet they did still bar him an exit visa in 1964 which prevented him from taking on the USA's Joey Giardello for the world middleweight title. Papp died aged 77 in October 2003, two years after being inducted into the International Boxing Hall of Fame.

STEVE REDGRAVE

An exhausted Steve Redgrave told TV crews after clinching his fourth Olympic gold in Atlanta 1996: "If anyone sees me going anywhere near a boat again, they have my permission to shoot me." Yet four years later he was on top of the winners' podium for a then-British record fifth time, this time in Sydney. Redgrave had overcome health setbacks such as being diagnosed with ulcerative colitis in 1992 and diabetes five years later. That coxless pairs victory in Atlanta, alongside Matthew Pinsent who would go on to end his career with four Olympic titles of his own, was Great Britain's solitary gold at the Atlanta Games. Redgrave was knighted in 2001 for services to rowing and was one of seven Olympic legends chosen to carry the torch inside London's Olympic Stadium in Stratford at the opening ceremony in 2012. His first Olympic gold, in Los Angeles in 1984, came in a boat with Martin Cross, Adrian Ellison, Andy Holmes and Richard Budgett, before he and Holmes teamed up for gold four years later, Pinsent accompanied him to glory in 1992 and 1996 and those two plus James Cracknell and Ed Coode triumphed in 2000. That last victory saw the British team lead from the start, yet they were closely pursued by their Italian rivals, with Redgrave and Co ultimately finishing in a time of 5:56.24 – marginally ahead of Italy's 5:56.62.

DAVID RUDISHA

Kenya's David Rudisha ran the 800m final in London 2012's Olympic Stadium as if it were a sprint, leading from the start and finishing in 1:40.91 minutes – ahead of silver medallist Nijel Amos of Botswana crossing the line in 1:41.73. Rudisha retained his title four years later in Rio, this time in 1:43.88 though only surging clear off the chasing field after the final turn. His London 2012 performance remains an 800m world record, with the next two best times being recorded by him too. Rudisha had initially favoured the 400m before being convinced by Irish coach Colm O'Connell to focus on the 800m instead. London 2012's organising committee chair Sebastian Coe – himself a double Olympic gold medallist, in the 1500m at Moscow 1980 and Los Angeles 1984 – described Rudisha's display in the English capital as his favourite of that summer's Games, calling it "the most extraordinary piece of running I have probably ever seen". Rudisha himself labelled the race "nice and easy". No one since has yet matched his feat of running the 800m in under one minute and 41 seconds. His father Daniel Rudisha was a member of Kenya's 4 x 400m silver medal-winning team at the 1968 Olympics in Mexico City.

TEÓFILO STEVENSON

Two men have gone on to emulate Hungary's László Papp in winning boxing gold medals at three Olympics in a row – and both came from Cuba. Teófilo Stevenson completed his hat-trick of heavyweight titles in Moscow in 1980, following on from triumphs in the same division at Munich 1972 and Montreal 1976. Stevenson, at 196cm, was a whole foot taller than Papp. He set his Olympic career off to the perfect start by knocking down Poland's Ludwik Denderys inside the opening 30 seconds of their first-round fight in Munich and went on to be given gold after his scheduled opponent in the final, Romania's Ion Alexe, had to miss out through injury. Stevenson turned down lucrative offers to go professional – despite the prospect of taking on Muhammad Ali – and remained amateur for his follow-up Olympic victories in 1976, beating Mircea Şimon of Romania in the final, and in 1980 where the USSR's Pyotr Zayev was seen off for gold. He was denied the chance to go for further medals at Los Angeles in 1984 and Seoul four years later as the Cuban government boycotted both Games. Stevenson retired in 1988 and died from a heart attack, aged 60, in the Cuban capital Havana in June 2012. The third boxer to win golds at three successive Olympics was fellow Cuban heavyweight Félix Savón, at Barcelona 1992, Atlanta 1996 and Sydney 2000.

OLYMPIC LEGENDS FROM THE REST OF THE WORLD

DALEY THOMPSON
🇬🇧 ●●

Francis "Daley" Thompson was a no-nonsense performer. After finishing 18th in the decathlon at the 1976 Olympics in Montreal, he went to the Moscow Games four years later having sent a postcard to the USA's double Olympic decathlon champion Bob Mathias vowing "I'm going for three!" Thompson would "only" emulate Mathias by winning two in a row, marking his second triumph at Los Angeles 1984 by running his victory lap after the final 1500m event in a top complaining about the host country's US bias in TV coverage. Thompson, the son of British Nigerian father Frank and Scottish mother Lydia, was given his nickname Daley from one of his middle names Ayodélé, meaning "joy come home". He switched to the decathlon as a teenager after failing in three individual athletics events at an amateur championships in 1974. He was helped in the decathlon by the fact that it started with his best two events, the 100m and long jump, but few would dispute his status as one of the greatest decathletes of all-time and certainly Great Britain's best. He broke the world record four times – including his 1984 Los Angeles tally of 8,798 points, having won 8,495 in Moscow – before finishing fourth at the 1988 Olympics in Seoul. True to his convention-challenging persona, Thompson collected his 1982 BBC Sports Personality of the Year award not in formal attire but instead in a tracksuit.

LAURA TROTT
🇬🇧 ●●●●●○

Laura Kenny, maiden name Trott, is the most successful Olympics cyclist of all time and the British woman with the most medals at the Games. She had been born a month premature and with a collapsed lung, before later being diagnosed with asthma, but took up cycling as a child alongside her mother who wanted to lose weight and Laura's elder sister Emma. Her major breakthrough came in the velodrome at London 2012, where she won team pursuit gold alongside Dani King and Joanna Rowsell in a world record time of 3:14.051 – and then another gold riding solo two days later, in the omnium. She retained both titles in Rio four years later, then at the Covid-19 pandemic-delayed Tokyo 2020 event in 2021 she added a fifth gold in the madison but had to settle for silver this time in the team pursuit, finishing six seconds behind the German team. No British woman before her had ever won gold medals at three Olympics in a row and she was chosen to carry the GB flag at the Tokyo 2020 closing ceremony. She and fellow cycling star Jason Kenny married in September 2016, not long after they had come home from Rio laden with yet more Olympic gold medals – Jason three that time to Laura's two.

BRADLEY WIGGINS

🇬🇧

Bradley Wiggins was already an accomplished and successful track cyclist, winning individual pursuit Olympic gold in Athens in 2004 before team pursuit and individual pursuit triumphs in Beijing four years later, when he added road cycling's ultimate honour in July 2012 – becoming Britain's first ever Tour de France champion. A mere week later he was sitting on a makeshift throne in the grounds of Hampton Court Palace after adding Olympic gold in the 27.3-mile time trial, finishing 42 seconds faster than Germany's silver medallist Tony Martin. His eight Olympic medals – the last of them team pursuit gold at Rio 2016 – are now only bettered by former team-mate Jason Kenny's nine. Wiggins, whose Australian father Gary had been a professional cyclist, is the first and so far only person to win the Tour de France and Olympic gold in the same year. He also rang the Olympic bell as part of London 2012's opening ceremony in the athletics stadium in Stratford, east London. Wiggins was made a Sir in 2013 though made light of the honour, saying he would only use the title for "comedy purposes". He retired from competitive cycling after the Rio 2016 Olympics though later competed in the following year's British Indoor Rowing Championships.

EMIL ZÁTOPEK

🇨🇿

Emil Zátopek made a sudden decision to run his first marathon on July 27 1952. He ended it winning Olympic gold, at the 1952 Helsinki Games – having already that summer successfully defended his 10,000m title from London 1948 and added 5,000m gold for good measure. Zátopek – dubbed the "Czech locomotive", and familiar for his ungainly running style and grimacing discomfort during races – was carried around the field by the Jamaican 4 x 400m relay team in Helsinki after completing his unprecedented hat-trick of long-distance golds at a single Olympics. He had been born on the very same day as his future wife Dana Zátopková, who herself won javelin gold at that 1952 Olympics – around the same time as Emil's 5,000m triumph – and then silver in the same event in Rome eight years later. Zátopek attempted to retain his marathon crown at Melbourne 1956 but finished sixth, hampered by a groin injury. Zátopek, a former lieutenant-colonel in the Czech army, was expelled from the country's Communist Party in 1968 after co-signing a pro-freedom letter and sent to work in a uranium mine, but was allowed to return to the capital Prague and reunite with his family in 1977. Prague's National Theatre hosted his funeral following his death at the age of 78 in November 2000 after suffering a stroke.